VICTORIA

BY

JOHN GUY

THE YOUNG VICTORIA

VICTORIA IS BORN

Victoria was born at Kensington Palace and was christened exactly one month later in the Cupola Room at the Palace. There was a dispute over her name, her parents eventually settling on Alexandrina Victoria as her registered name, but they called her Victoria from birth.

*W*hen Victoria was born on 24 May 1819 she was fifth in line to the throne and the likelihood of her succeeding seemed very remote. Her grandfather, George III, was still king and ahead of her in succession were her uncles, George, the Prince Regent, the Dukes of York and Clarence, and of course her father, the Duke of Kent. Within a short space of time, however, all that changed. Her father died unexpectedly on 23 January 1820 followed, six days later, by her grandfather. The Duke of York died in 1827, taking her a step nearer the throne. Her remaining uncles succeeded as George IV and William IV, respectively, but their failing health produced no heirs, leaving Victoria as heir to the throne.

PERSONAL POSSESSIONS

Many of Queen Victoria's personal possessions still survive, a number of them on view at the Victoria and Albert Museum. These reading glasses once belonged to the Queen; the case is inscribed with her personal insignia.

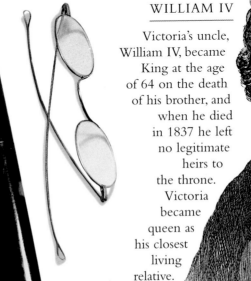

WILLIAM IV

Victoria's uncle, William IV, became King at the age of 64 on the death of his brother, and when he died in 1837 he left no legitimate heirs to the throne. Victoria became queen as his closest living relative.

THE YOUNG PRINCESS

Always a friendly and playful child (who had no fewer than 132 dolls!), she had an aptitude for music, singing and dancing and was an accomplished artist. She spoke with a strong German accent as a child, because of her mother's German origins, and she could speak German and French fluently.

THE QUEEN COMES OF AGE

Princess Victoria was just 18 years old when she heard of the death of her uncle, William IV, in 1837. She was immediately filled with feelings of both happiness and sadness, but seems to have assumed the awesome responsibility with apparent calm. She was crowned the following year, on 28 June, at Westminster Abbey. Not a popular figure at first, she was destined to become Britain's longest reigning monarch and ruler over the greatest empire the world has ever seen.

DUCHESS OF KENT

Victoria's father was Edward, Duke of Kent, fourth son of George III. Victoria never knew her father, who died when she was a baby. Her mother, the Duchess of Kent, was appointed Regent in case Victoria succeeded to the throne whilst still a child.

PRINCE ALBERT

One of the first dilemmas facing Victoria when she succeeded to the throne was that of marriage. Lord Melbourne, the Prime Minister, advised Victoria to marry as soon as possible to create her own heirs. At first she had no interest in doing so but agreed to meet her cousin, Prince Albert of Saxe-Coburg-Gotha. Both entered the relationship reluctantly at first, but there seems to have been a mutual attraction and they soon became very dear friends. After marriage their friendship developed into a very deep and genuine love for one another and they became a devoted couple.

THE PRINCE CONSORT

Prince Albert was, in Victoria's own words, *'so sensible, so kind, and so good, and so amiable...the most pleasing and delightful exterior and appearance you can possibly see.'* He was tall, intelligent and proved to be a very able political adviser to Victoria. He took a genuine interest in his new adoptive country, particularly the poorer classes. He is credited with re-introducing the practice of bringing decorated Christmas trees into the house, a custom still practised in his native Germany, though it had long fallen out of favour in England.

THE ROYAL WEDDING

The wedding between Victoria and Albert took place on 10 February 1840 at St. James's Palace. They were both just 20 years old. She wore a white satin gown with a lace flounce, and a Turkish diamond necklace and sapphire brooch (a present from Albert). The couple were well received by the public. After the wedding reception held at Buckingham Palace, they had a three-day honeymoon at Windsor Castle.

THE PRINCE DIES

In 1861 Prince Albert contracted typhoid and died prematurely, at the age of 42. The Queen was heartbroken. The prospect of facing the world alone culminated in a nervous breakdown. She wore black for the rest of her life in respect for Albert. At first the public sympathized with her, but after over a decade of mourning, there were calls for her abdication.

THE QUEEN PROPOSES

According to the dictates of royal protocol, no man is allowed to propose to a queen, so Victoria had to ask for Albert's hand in marriage. She proposed to him on 15 October 1839. In her diary, Victoria wrote that Albert's acceptance was the brightest and happiest moment of her life.

KEEPSAKES

To commemorate the royal wedding a great many mementoes were made, such as this decorative lustre-ware jug.

EVENTS OF VICTORIA'S LIFE

~1819~
Victoria born at Kensington Palace

~1820~
Victoria's father Edward, Duke of Kent, dies

~1830~
George IV dies

William IV accedes to the throne

~1832~
First Reform Act passed to reform parliamentary system

~1833~
Slavery abolished throughout the Empire

~1834~
Poor Law creates workhouses for the poor

Houses of Parliament burn down

~1837~
William IV dies

Victoria accedes to the throne

~1838~
Victoria's coronation

People's Charter issued, calling for political reform

~1839~
First camera developed

~1840~
Victoria marries Albert of Saxe-Coburg-Gotha

FAMILY LIFE

*V*ictoria is often pictured as a stern, austere woman, an image perpetuated by her choice to wear black for so many years after Albert's death. She is seldom seen smiling in pictures, but supposedly was a jovial person. One reason for her glum expressions was possibly the slow film speed used by photographers at the time. Subjects often had to hold a pose for 30 seconds (or longer) so as not to blur the image, making it difficult to hold a smile. Historians have often concentrated on the more serious side to Victoria's personality, neglecting her love of life, particularly family life. She was amused by the antics of children and both she and Albert enjoyed simple, family pastimes. In later life, Victoria loved to see herself as the great matriarch.

SOFTLY, SOFTLY

Contrary to popular opinion, Victoria was not a strict authoritarian. She preferred to instruct her children by setting a good moral example rather than to over-discipline them.

THE GRANDMOTHER OF EUROPE

This picture, taken in 1897, shows the extended family of Queen Victoria. The Prince of Wales (and future king Edward VII) stands immediately to her left. By the various marriages of her children and grand-children, Victoria was related to all of the major royal houses of Europe, including Germany, Norway, Sweden, Greece, Spain, Romania and Russia, earning her the affectionate title 'the grandmother of Europe'.

~1840~
Penny postal service
introduced

Princess 'Vicky'
born (Victoria's
first child)

~1841~
Sir Robert Peel
becomes Prime
Minister

~1845~
Beginning of Irish
potato famine

~1846~
Corn Laws repealed

~1851~
Great Exhibition in
London, initiated by
Prince Albert

~1853~
Vaccination against
smallpox made
compulsory

Albert begins rebuilding
Balmoral Castle to his
own designs

~1854~
Crimean War breaks
out between Britain
(and France)
and Russia

~1856~
Victoria Cross first
introduced for bravery
in wartime

~1857~
Indian Mutiny against
British rule

HAPPY FAMILIES

In keeping with most families of the day, Victoria and Albert had many children, nine in all. She gave birth to Princess Victoria (Vicky) in November 1840. Vicky, the Princess Royal, remained a close friend throughout the Queen's life, especially after Albert's death. Victoria's family life was, by all accounts, a happy one. It is difficult to say what kind of relationship she had with all her children: some accounts claim she was aloof and dispassionate, others paint a rosier picture. There does appear to have been real animosity between her and Edward, the future king, whom she thought foolish, and was critical of his behaviour.

PERSONAL RECOLLECTIONS

We know a great deal about the personal life and opinions of Queen Victoria from her diary, which she maintained throughout her life. It was not, as many suppose, a secret diary, certainly not in her younger years, because it was frequently perused by her mother and governess.

ASSASSINATION ATTEMPTS

At the beginning of her reign Victoria was not a popular figure at all. As ruling monarch, she was often seen as the cause of social discontent; some would have preferred a king on the throne. There were several attempts made on Victoria's life including this attempt in 1840 by Edward Oxford.

REFORM ACTS

During her reign, Victoria approved several Acts of Parliament that had important social and constitutional implications. Growing unrest in Britain meant new political movements were forcing change. In 1838 the Chartists issued the 'Peoples' Charter' which called for political reform. Although not fully realized until 1944, it forms the basis of our parliamentary system today. In 1867 and 1884, the Second and Third Reform Acts extended the right to vote to more people.

FATHER FIGURE

During the early years of her reign Victoria relied heavily on the advice of Lord Melbourne, the Whig (Liberal) Prime Minister, who guided her through the intricacies of politics and her role in government.

SOCIAL CHANGE

The Industrial Revolution saw Britain change from a mainly agricultural nation to an industrial one. People who left the country to seek employment in the towns were exploited by greedy industrialists. Trade unionists like Joseph Arch, founder of the National Union of Farm Labourers (shown right), fought a long and hard battle for workers' rights. Trade unions were finally legalized in 1871.

VICTORIA & GOVERNMENT

From the beginning Victoria showed a genuine interest in the government of the country and developed a good rapport with most of the leading politicians of the day. She took her role seriously and, whilst accepting the relatively new idea of a constitutional monarchy (which meant that she had no real part to play in politics), she also realized that she had considerable influence and exercised her powers wisely. Albert, who had shown little interest in politics prior to their marriage, also took an active role in matters of government.

POLITICAL GIANTS

Victoria witnessed the coming and going of several great politicians, including William Gladstone and Benjamin Disraeli. Victoria liked Disraeli (above) and had him invested Earl of Beaconsfield, whereas Gladstone frequently incurred her wrath.

A NEW HOUSE FOR PARLIAMENT

Until the reign of Victoria's uncle, William IV, Parliament met in the old royal palace of Westminster. Like most medieval buildings, it contained a lot of wood and burned down in a disastrous fire in 1834. The present Houses of Parliament were rebuilt on part of the old palace site. Victoria officiated at the opening of the new building in 1867.

LIFE EXPECTANCY

This picture shows a father comforting his dying child. Childhood deaths were not uncommon in Victorian Britain. There was no National Health Service and the poor could rarely afford medical treatment. In the country the life expectancy was around 50, but for those living in squalid conditions in towns many were lucky to reach 40.

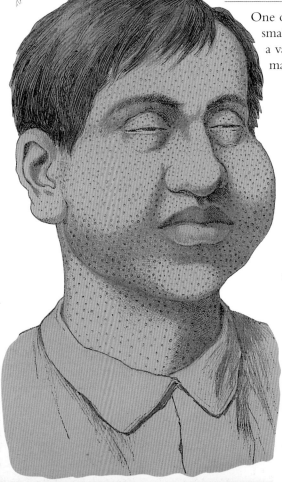

SMALLPOX

One of the most contagious and deadly diseases was smallpox. The scientist, Edward Jenner, pioneered a vaccine to combat the disease. Vaccination was made compulsory in 1853.

SANITATION

Many of the diseases prevalent in Victorian Britain were caused through poor sanitation and living conditions. A series of Public Health Acts after 1848 made it the responsibility of local councils to provide proper drainage and clean water supplies.

Only the rich could afford the luxury of an indoor toilet. The poor had to make do with open cesspits in the backyard or, worse still, a communal toilet shared by up to 100 others.

LIFE IN VICTORIAN ENGLAND

A t the beginning of Victoria's reign (1837), the population of Britain was about 20 million, only 20 per cent of whom lived in towns. The rest still managed to eke out a living from the land. By the end of her reign (1901) the population had doubled with over 75 per cent living in towns. These burgeoning populations meant that row upon row of poor-quality terraced slums were erected around the factories. Living conditions were appalling and disease was rife, particularly water-borne diseases such as cholera and typhoid.

POSTAL SERVICE

No proper postal service had existed in Britain until 1840 when the Penny Post was introduced. This revolutionized the delivery of letters and for just 1d. (0.4p) a letter could be sent anywhere in the country. The first stamp issued was the Penny Black. It carried a profile of the Queen, a tradition adopted throughout the Empire and still maintained today.

WORK ETHIC

Workhouses were first introduced in 1834 and were often the only help available for the poor and homeless in Victorian towns. People received basic food and lodging in return for work, often in extremely harsh conditions.

SOCIAL HISTORIAN

Charles Dickens (1812-70) was the greatest and most popular novelist of his day. Many of his novels, such as *Oliver Twist*, paint a vivid description of life in Victorian Britain and he was often regarded as a champion of the poor.
Victoria started to accept Dickens's picture of Britain when her own beloved husband died of typhoid, contracted most probably from the open sewers around Windsor.

ART & INVENTIONS

The speed at which new inventions and discoveries appeared in Victorian Britain was phenomenal. These developments changed the way people had been living almost overnight. The first electric light bulbs were invented in America by Thomas Edison who, in 1877, also invented the phonograph (forerunner of modern hi-fi). The telephone was invented in 1875 by another American, Alexander Graham Bell. Food processing and packaging in tins kept food fresh for longer. Many items, however, were still relatively expensive and so were enjoyed only by the wealthy.

PHOTOGRAPHIC RECORD

Victoria's was the first reign in history to be fully documented in photographs. The first primitive photographic images were produced in 1800. The first camera, as shown here, was developed by William Fox Talbot in 1839.

THE MEDICINE MEN

The Victorian Age was one of great learning, a period when great minds collaborated to push the bounds of human knowledge to the limits. Doctors such as Joseph Lister recognized that bacteria were the cause of infection. He developed an antiseptic in 1867. Prior to that, chloroform had been developed for use as an anaesthetic during operations. Victoria herself was administered chloroform during the birth of her last child, Beatrice, in 1857.

ARTISTIC LICENCE

It has often been said that the Victorians did not have an architectural style of their own, but merely borrowed from past eras. In fact, their use of cast iron and glass is a style wholly their own. In more traditional buildings they freely interpreted a variety of styles, such as medieval, to create 'Victorian Gothick', as seen here at Cardiff Castle.

GRANDIOSE IDEAS

The Victorians built on a monumental scale. They erected the largest buildings then known, reflecting the bold confidence of the new industrial age. The use of cast iron and glass made it possible to span huge floor areas. This view shows the railway station at St. Pancras under construction.

AGE OF SCIENCE

Michael Faraday's experiments with electro-magnetism realized the full potential of electricity as a major power source. Eager to promote the use of new technologies, Queen Victoria had electric lighting installed in all her palaces. She also demonstrated this new technology during her Diamond Jubilee celebrations in 1897 by pressing an electric button that was connected to a telegraph. It transmitted a message throughout the Empire, beginning the tradition of the royal broadcast on Christmas Day.

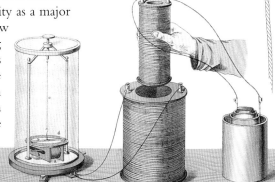

EVENTS OF
VICTORIA'S LIFE

~1859~
Charles Darwin publishes
Origin of the Species

~1861~
Prince Albert dies
of typhoid

Victoria goes into
mourning and withdraws
from public life

~1863~
Edward, Prince of Wales
(Victoria's eldest son and
heir) marries Alexandra
of Denmark

~1867~
Canada becomes first
country within British
Empire to be declared
an independent
dominion

Second Reform
Bill passed; further
parliamentary reforms

New Houses of
Parliament opened

~1868~
Gladstone becomes
Prime Minister

JOSEPH PAXTON

The Crystal Palace building was designed by Joseph Paxton, a brilliant engineer who had erected huge conservatories at stately homes, but this was his masterpiece. It was truly a wonder of the age and prompted Queen Victoria to call it a 'fairy-tale palace'. Paxton received the fee of £5,000 (which is the equivalent of £1 million today) for designing and building it.

THE GREAT EXHIBITION

The Great Exhibition of 1851 was the brainchild of Prince Albert. He believed that an international exhibition in London would both act as a shop window for British industry and generate more work to benefit the poor. His ideas were not met with enthusiasm by the government but, undaunted, he won popular support and private finance through the press. The exhibition was opened on 1 May 1851 by Queen Victoria and was a resounding success. From then, until its closure on 15 October, over six million people visited the exhibition at a time when Britain's population was only about 20 million. It was the first international trade exhibition in the world.

PREFABRICATED BUILDING

The Crystal Palace, shown here during its original construction, was made of prefabricated parts which enabled the building to be taken down after the exhibition closed in Hyde Park and re-erected some miles away at Sydenham in 1854. The area is still known as Crystal Palace. Sadly, the building burned down in a disastrous fire in 1936.

FROM FAR AND WIDE

Inside the exhibition building there were over 14,000 different exhibitors, over half of whom were from the British Empire. Industrialists from across the globe came to view the best of British industry and place orders for all manner of commodities, from steam trains to spinning machines, textiles to fine art. Admission charges were reduced after two days to ensure that people of all classes could attend.

MUSEUMS FOR ALL

Albert determined that the ordinary people of Britain should benefit from the exhibition; money raised from the proceeds was used to open several large museums in London. These included the Victoria and Albert, the Science and the Natural History Museums, which collectively became the envy of the world.

THE CRYSTAL PALACE

The original exhibition building, erected at Hyde Park, was a masterpiece of cast iron and glass, earning it the title 'The Crystal Palace'. It covered an area of 26 acres and was three times the size of St. Paul's Cathedral. It was about 550 metres (600 yards) long and contained over 300,000 individual panes of glass.

WORKSHOP OF THE WORLD

MAN OF GENIUS

Throughout the Victorian era there were men of exceptional genius and vision. Isambard Kingdom Brunel was such a man. A brilliant and innovative engineer, he specialized in the use of iron and steel in his designs for ships and civil engineering projects. His revolutionary liner, the *Great Britain,* was launched by Prince Albert in 1843; the biggest ship ever built.

The Victorians believed that work was a virtue and was good for the soul – none more than Victoria herself, whose own workload was quite prodigious. Technological developments were faster in Britain than anywhere else in the world. Britain had been the first to embrace the new 'industrial revolution' sweeping the developed countries, earning it the title 'Workshop of the World'.

WORKING CONDITIONS

The working class bore the brunt of the rapid industrialization. People used to rural outdoor life now had to work in mines and factories, often some distance away from their homes and in cramped and airless conditions.

THE PRICE OF PROGRESS

One of the worst aspects of town life was the pollution that resulted from burning large quantities of fossil fuels, such as coal. Victoria increasingly found life in London intolerable and spent long periods in the country.

CHILD LABOUR

Women and children were used to working on farms, but in industrial Britain they were forced to work long hours in appalling conditions. Fourteen hours a day was quite usual and factory owners would employ children as young as five.

WHEEL OF FORTUNE

The industrialization of Britain and the strength of the Empire were of mutual benefit. The new industries sold their products to the colonies, and in turn, the colonies supplied Britain with endless raw materials to make yet more goods. So the cycle continued. A large merchant fleet was essential for the transportation of these goods, and Britain had the largest navy to protect the merchant ships.

RAILWAYS

At the beginning of Victoria's reign there were about 3,200 kilometres (2,000 miles) of railway in Britain. By 1870 this figure had grown to 22,000 kilometres (13,750 miles). At first there was strong resistance to railways, especially from canal owners, but 'railway mania' soon erupted. Branch lines opened up all over the country, transporting goods cheaply and quickly from the factories to the ports.

FIRST COLONIES

The British Empire began as a small collection of colonies along the eastern coast of North America. They formed themselves into 13 states, and gained their independence in the reign of Victoria's grandfather, George III. Colonies were also established in what is now Canada during a search for a north-west passage to Asia.

THE MILITARY

Although Britain's Empire was not primarily military led, countries subjected to British rule were held down by a strong military presence.

THE INDIAN MUTIN

Since the 18th century, the East India Company had employed Indian troops. In 1857, these native troops rebelled and a series of bloody battles ensued. The mutiny was eventually crushed and India came under the direct rule of the British Government. In 1876, Victoria became Empress of India, a title all future monarchs retained until India received its independence in 1947.

THE EAST INDIA COMPANY

Elizabethan mariners first landed in India in the 16th century, opening a number of trade routes. In 1600, the East India Company was set up to protect British interests in India and develop further trading contacts with Asia.

THE BRITISH EMPIRE . . .

By the end of Victoria's reign she presided over the largest empire that the world had ever seen. Always conscious of her position as its monarchical head, Victoria was greatly responsible for creating the 'family of nations', later known as the Commonwealth. Unlike other past empires, the interests of the British Empire lay with trade and the wealth it generated, rather than world domination. Although aided by the military, it was not military led, and colonies were acquired in a piecemeal fashion, stretching across the globe.

ORIGINS OF THE EMPIRE

The origins of the British Empire can be traced to the reign of Elizabeth I. In Elizabeth's time, England was often at war with other European nations, particularly Spain who controlled all the major trade routes to the Americas and the East. A series of voyages to uncharted areas of the world became quests for new trade routes and land to establish new colonies.

ROBERT CLIVE

Britain's rule in India began with the victory of Robert Clive in 1757. He defeated the massive combined Indo-French army of 60,000 with a small force of 3,000 men, securing the province of Bengal. Although regarded as a hero back in Britain, Clive was understandably hated by the Indians.

EXTENT OF THE EMPIRE

This map shows the extent of the British Empire (coloured orange) in 1886. All of the major trading routes were under British control, which explains why Britain was such a major influence throughout the world.

EQUAL PORTIONS

Throughout the 18th and 19th centuries there was considerable land-hunger amongst the major world powers. They had the attitude that the world was theirs for the taking and had little regard for the native peoples. This cartoon shows various heads of state dividing up China like a piece of pie, while the Chinese leader looks on helplessly.

BRITISH WAY OF LIFE

When subjugating a new land, the British forced the native people to adopt British ways. Official buildings and houses were built in British styles and British legal and government systems were introduced. The English language became widely-spoken and remains the most dominant language in the world.

THE BRITISH EMPIRE . . .

The raising of the Union Jack to denote British sovereignty over a newly acquired country was always treated with a great deal of reverence, accompanied by much pomp and ceremony.

The British Empire grew slowly. At its fullest extent it covered one quarter of the world's land mass. It reached its zenith immediately after the First World War, when the former German colonies in Africa and Asia were taken over. Because its colonies were scattered across the globe, resources were eventually stretched too thinly. The military were unable to cope and when Britain began to have economic problems at home, the Empire gradually went into decline.

VOYAGES OF DISCOVERY

In Elizabethan times, the motives for exploration were quite simple: gold and new trade routes. By Victoria's reign, it was commonplace for explorers to take scientists with them on their voyages, to record and bring back samples of new plants and animal species for scientific study. This practice was started by explorers such as James Cook who is seen here raising the Union Jack in New South Wales, Australia, in 1770.

THE BRITISH EMPIRE

EMPRESS OF INDIA

In 1876 Queen Victoria was proclaimed Empress of India and was proud to accept the title. She is seen here, in this contemporary cartoon, being asked by Prime Minister Disraeli to trade the imperial crown of India for her own.

*T*he reign of Victoria was a golden era, a time when even the Queen herself believed that the 'sun would never set on the Empire'. It coincided with a period of great social and economic change, when Britain led the world in science and technology. Although the British government exploited the colonies, many of them benefited from Britain's developments. Many of the world's railway systems, for example, were built by British engineers, and commodities made in Britain were exported all over the globe. In short, Britain took the world by storm.

FRESH START

One of the strengths of the British Empire lay in colonizing subjugated nations with British citizens. Like these emigrants bound for Sydney, many were keen to try a fresh start in the colonies, faced with poverty and unemployment at home.

THE GERMAN THREAT

The main threat to the Empire came, not from rebelling colonies, but from Germany; more specifically from Victoria's own grandson, Kaiser Wilhelm II. Although Britain's navy was by far the greatest in the world, Germany was able to build warships of the very latest design at a faster rate than Britain could replace its obsolete ones.

BRITANNIA RULES THE WAVES

Four days after Victoria's Diamond Jubilee, in 1897, the Royal Navy staged a massive display of its power at Spithead, on the south coast. It was the largest collection of warships ever assembled and demonstrated to the world the might of the British Empire.

SLAVERY ABOLISHED

Slavery was abolished throughout the Empire in 1833, some years before Victoria's reign. The treatment of native peoples from the colonies was a matter close to the Queen's heart. She strongly resisted giving the Boers of South Africa their independence, for example, fearing they would treat the natives too harshly.

ÉVÉNEMENTS DU TRANSVAAL
Sommation aux Anglais

BRITAIN AT WAR

*T*hroughout Victoria's reign, as Britain greatly extended its empire, there were a number of imperial conflicts. With rising unemployment at home, there was no shortage of manpower to join the ranks of the army. Like Britain, all the other major powers in Europe were keen to acquire new colonies. This jostling for supremacy and land was the cause of one of the worst conflicts in history: the First World War.

BADEN-POWELL

The flamboyant Lieutenant-Colonel, Robert Baden-Powell, became a national hero during the Boer War. He made the small South African trading post of Mafeking his military headquarters and held the town, against 8,000 Boers, with just 1,000 soldiers, losing only 35 men. Baden-Powell went on to form the Boy Scout movement in 1908.

THE BOER WAR (1899-1902)

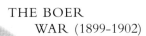

The Boers were South African farmers (descended from Dutch settlers) who fiercely resisted Britain's attempts to annexe South Africa after the discovery of gold there. They used guerrilla tactics to combat the massive British force sent against them, but eventually the sheer size of the British army crushed their resistance.

THE CRIMEAN WAR (1854-56)

The Crimean War was fought between Britain and Russia on a peninsula that is now part of modern-day Turkey. Britain was unprepared for the scale of the conflict and suffered one of its worst military disasters, the 'Charge of the Light Brigade', at Balaclava in 1854.

FLORENCE NIGHTINGALE

Florence Nightingale (the 'Lady of the Lamp') is best remembered for her work in the Crimean War, tending to the injuries of wounded soldiers. Her reports of the horrors of the Crimea sent shock waves that were felt throughout society. Afterwards, she devoted her life to the better training of nurses.

THE VICTORIA CROSS

During the Crimean War, Victoria had a special medal struck for those who had served in the war. She insisted that no distinction be made between officers and privates – a revolutionary step for the day. She later created the Victoria Cross which is still the highest military honour accorded today.

THE ROYAL PALACES

BUCKINGHAM PALACE

The population census of 1841 shows Buckingham Palace to be Queen Victoria's main residence. It is still the residence most often associated with British royalty but is a relative newcomer to the list of royal palaces. Victoria's grandfather, George III, purchased the house for £28,000 in 1762. The state apartments are magnificent, and frequently host state functions.

Victoria and Albert made full use of the royal palaces. For official duties, balls and government functions they favoured Buckingham Palace (shown here in 1852), but the Queen always preferred the privacy of Windsor Castle. As a young girl Victoria enjoyed the hurly-burly of London's social scene, but Albert was a country man at heart, preferring the peace and solitude of the country estates. Later in life, Victoria also came to prefer them.

OSBORNE HOUSE

In 1844, Victoria and Albert began looking for a house to which they could retire from the hustle and bustle of court life. The Osborne estate on the Isle of Wight proved ideal, and Prince Albert designed and built a new house in Italian Renaissance style.

BALMORAL CASTLE

This view shows part of Victoria's private apartments (the drawing room) at Balmoral Castle in Aberdeenshire. Surrounded by mountains and set in 30,000 acres of deer forest, Balmoral has always been a royal favourite since it was purchased and redesigned by Prince Albert in 1853.

WINDSOR CASTLE

Windsor Castle is the oldest royal residence in Britain and also the largest inhabited castle in the world. Begun by William the Conqueror in 1066 it has been greatly extended since then. Successive monarchs, right up to George IV, Victoria's uncle, continued the process of transforming the great medieval castle into a magnificent palace.

THE JUBILEE YEARS

MEMENTOES OF A SPECIAL DAY

For Victoria's Golden and Diamond Jubilees, many people were given the day off work and most remembered the day by buying specially-made souvenirs.

T he last years of Victoria's reign were a marked contrast to the early years. Although she eventually came out of mourning for Albert some 13 years after his death (in 1874), she never got over his loss. She returned to public life, but with advancing years the queen became a sadder, more melancholic person. Victoria had not been universally popular throughout her reign. Many had not welcomed her to the throne, but by the time of her Golden Jubilee in 1887 she was at the height of her popularity.

NEVER-TO-BE-FORGOTTEN DAY

The Queen's Golden Jubilee marked 50 years of her reign. People throughout the Empire celebrated the event, particularly in Britain itself (and more especially in London) with wild enthusiasm. Victoria said of the occasion: *'This never-to-be-forgotten day will always leave the most gratifying and heart-stirring memories behind.'*

FAMILY GATHERING

On the occasion of her Golden Jubilee, Victoria attended a banquet held in her honour in Buckingham Palace. Invited guests included all the crowned heads of Europe, most of whom were related to Victoria. For her Diamond Jubilee in 1897, as this portrait shows, the gathering was of her 'extended family' and colonial premiers from countries throughout the Empire.

THE DIAMOND JUBILEE

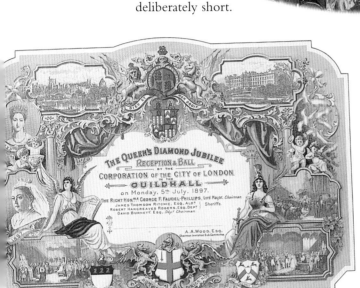

This painting shows Queen Victoria arriving at St. Paul's Cathedral for a thanksgiving service on 22 June 1897, held in honour of her Diamond Jubilee. Out of respect for her age and ailing health the service was kept deliberately short.

ROYAL INVITE

This picture shows one of the formal invitations to the Queen's Diamond Jubilee celebrations at the Guildhall in London, one of many public functions held throughout the country. By this time the Queen was a frail old lady with bad rheumatism and failing eyesight, confined to a wheelchair. However, she continued to perform her duties right up until a few weeks before she died.

THE END OF AN ERA

FAMILY FEUDS

This family tree shows that most of Victoria's children married into the royal houses of Europe, which she hoped would have a stabilizing effect on European politics. Sadly, this was not to be.

*W*ith the death of Victoria on 22 January 1901, it really was the end of an era. In some respects Victoria was liberal in her attitude, taking a keen interest in improving the living conditions of the poor, but in other ways she was very conservative. She frowned upon the idea of women holding professions, yet she objected strongly to the working conditions imposed on women and children in the mines and factories. Similarly, she opposed giving the vote to women, but supported giving the vote to working class men. Britain had seen more change during her reign than in any other period in history, but the world was now poised on the threshold of a whole new age.

THREAT TO PEACE

This picture shows the Kaiser, William II, Victoria's grandson by the marriage of her daughter Vicky to Prince Frederick of Prussia. Victoria always resented his anti-British views, but he was at her bedside when she lay dying. Had she lived a few more years she would have seen him lead Germany against Britain in the First World War.

PROBLEM CHILD

This view shows Victoria with her son, the future King Edward VII, shortly before her death. She was always critical of Edward and did not feel he had the necessary qualities to make a good king. She deliberately kept him out of government issues for fear his head-strong attitude might create problems. In later life she finally acknowledged him as her heir.

TRUSTED ADVISER

Victoria followed a high moral code in life, but she was no stranger to scandal. During her period of mourning for Albert she befriended a Scots servant called John Brown, an excellent horseman, who the Queen trusted and took into her confidence. He became her constant companion and rumours began to circulate they were having an affair, causing her popularity to sink to an all-time low.

FAMILY PORTRAIT

This family portrait was taken at Osborne House in 1898, three years before Victoria's death. When she died, her body was taken from there to Cowes and on to London. Her funeral was carried out according to her own instructions and she was buried at Frogmore, sharing the same mausoleum as her beloved husband, Prince Albert.

EVENTS OF VICTORIA'S LIFE

~1887~
Independent Labour Party founded

~1897~
Victoria's Diamond Jubilee celebrates 60 years on the throne

Spithead naval review

~1899~
Boer War breaks out in South Africa

~1900~
Victoria's son, Alfred, dies

~1901~
Queen Victoria dies; our longest reigning monarch

Edward VII accedes to the throne

DID YOU KNOW?

That until Victoria's reign only the rich could afford to drink tea? Although it seems difficult to believe now, the humble cup of tea, the most popular drink in Britain today, used to be a luxury that few could afford. When the Empire expanded, tea was imported in bulk, from India and China, making it affordable by all classes for the first time.

That the Scouts movement had its origins in the Boer War? In 1908 Robert Baden-Powell published a small pamphlet entitled *Scouting for Boys*. It marked the beginnings of the scouting movement and soon boys were queuing up to join, attracted by the exciting world of adventure, camping and outdoor activities described in the booklet. Baden-Powell based many of the scouts activities directly on army life in South Africa, even copying the uniform from that worn by the military in hot climates.

That Charles Darwin suffered public derision and ill-health as a result of publishing his book *The Origin of the Species?* When Charles Darwin first published his famous book on evolution (on which most modern thought on evolution is derived) in 1859, there was a public outcry. Until then, many people believed in the literal truth of the Old Testament, especially the account of God's creation of the Earth. Darwin's revolutionary theories of natural selection were publicly criticized and he was accused of blasphemy by fellow scholars and eminent churchmen. Darwin was forced to challenge his own religious beliefs and was so overcome with guilt at daring to call into question Biblical authority that he became physically ill.

That the Brontë sisters adopted male names to avoid prejudice against women? The three Brontë sisters, Charlotte, Emily and Anne, amongst the most celebrated of Victorian novelists, were forced to use male pseudonyms in order to get their work published. They used the names Currer, Acton and Ellis Bell, respectively. The Brontës lonely life on the Yorkshire moors is reflected in their haunting novels, particularly Charlotte's *Jane Eyre* and Emily's *Wuthering Heights*. They all died within seven years of one another, all at very young ages.

That Railway timetables provided the first 'standard' time throughout Britain? Prior to the expansion of the railway system in Victorian times, people in Britain set their clocks by the position of the sun. This meant that clocks in the far west of the country showed a slightly different time to those in the east. This made it difficult for train drivers and signalmen, who needed to know the precise time of a train's arrival. A standard 'railway time', based on Greenwich meantime in London, was introduced at all railway stations and this eventually became accepted by everyone across the country as 'standard time'.

ACKNOWLEDGEMENTS

We would like to thank: Graham Rich, Rosalind Beckman and Elizabeth Wiggans for their assistance.

Copyright © 1998 ticktock Publishing Ltd.

First published in Great Britain by ticktock Publishing Ltd., Century Place, Lamberts Road. Tunbridge Wells, Kent, TN2 3EH.

No part of this publication may be reproduced, stored in a retrieval system, or transmitted in any form or by any means electronic, mechanical, photocopying, recording or otherwise, without prior written permission of the copyright owner.

A CIP catalogue record for this book is available from the British Library. ISBN 1 86007 033 7

Picture research by Image Select.

Printed in Hong Kong.

Picture Credits:

t=top, b=bottom, c=centre, l=left, r=right, OFC=outside front cover, IFC=inside front cover, OBC=outside back cover, IBC=inside back cover

Ann Ronan at Image Select International Ltd; OBC - right, 2tl, 2br, 4r, 5c, 6bl, 6tl, 8tr, 8c, 9tr, 9bl & OFC, 10bl & OBC, 10br, 10t, 11br, 11tr & OBC, 12bl, 13br, 13c, 14tl, 14bl, 16br, 16tl & OBC, 16/17c & OFC, 17t, 17br, 18l, 18/19c, 19tr, 21b, 22b, 22tl, 23tl, 23tr, 24bl, 24/25cb, 25cr & 25br, 30tl, 31tr. The Bridgeman Art Library, London; OBC - bottom left, 3br, 3tl, 3t, 4l & OFC, 5bl, 7tl, 8bl, 11cb, 12tl, 13tl, 15tl, 16bl, 18/19cb, 20t, 20bl, 23bl & 23br, 26/27 (main image), 27tr, 28bl & OFC (main image), 28tl & OFC, 29cl, 30/31c. Bridgeman - Giraudon; IFC & 29r. Chris Fairclough Colour Library at Image Select International Ltd; 9br, 27c. The Fotomas Index (London); 2bl, 6/7cb, 19br. By Courtesy of Fine Art Photographic Library; 25t. Image Select International Ltd; 12/13c, 14/15c, 18tr,, 26tl, 30/31cb, 30bl. Mary Evans Picture Library, London; 5tl, 15br, 20br & OFC, 24tl, 32c & OFC, 26/27c, 29b. Spectrum Colour Library; 21tr.

Every effort has been made to trace the copyright holders and we apologize in advance for any unintentional omissions. We would be pleased to insert the appropriate acknowledgement in any subsequent edition of this publication.

snapping-turtle guide

VICTORIAN LIFE

BY

JOHN GUY

COUNTRY LIFE

*W*hile new technology and machinery improved the efficiency and profitability of many farms, for most people the industrial revolution of the 18th and 19th centuries was a period of massive upheaval and social change. Many people lost their jobs and their homes, since most houses were tied to their occupations and they were forced to seek work elsewhere.

NEW MACHINERY

New machinery, such as this steam traction engine, was very versatile and could do the work of several men. In the space of a few years the heavy horses, that formerly pulled ploughs and other agricultural machinery, became obsolete.

ANIMAL HUSBANDRY

While those involved in agriculture suffered enormously at the hands of 'progress', many of those who tended animals, such as cattle herders and shepherds, were little affected by the technological revolution sweeping the land; survivors from a pre-industrial age.

COUNTRY AIR

Although many of those who worked in the country still lived in primitive, one-roomed cottages, living conditions and sanitation were much better than in town slums.

CHANGING MARKETPLACE

Many villages lost their weekly market as more and more of the food produced was taken to the towns to feed their burgeoning populations. A single village shop, selling a range of goods, could usually satisfy the needs of most rural communities.

LIFE EXPECTANCY

Although generally less well-off than town dwellers, those who lived in the country usually had a better quality of life and could expect to live longer; about 50 years of age compared to 40 for those in towns.

OUR DAILY BREAD

In 1815 Corn Laws had been passed to keep grain prices high and protect England from cheap imports, but these were repealed in 1846 to facilitate free trade. The result was a fall in the price of bread, though farmers were affected badly as a consequence.

LIFE IN TOWNS

At the beginning of Victoria's reign (1837) only about 20% of the population lived in towns, but by 1901, when she died, this figure had risen to about 75%. During this period the population of Britain doubled from around 20 million to 40 million. Most people moved to towns to find work in the factories, Rows of poor quality terraced slums sprang up around the factories to house them.

VICTIMS OF CIRCUMSTANCE

Poverty was so bad in most towns that many people resorted to crime in the dingy streets. The old and infirm, particularly, often fell victim to pickpockets.

POOR SANITATION

Sanitary conditions in Victorian towns were often very poor. Only the rich could afford proper toilet facilities. The poor had to share a communal lavatory, usually just a shed over a hole in the ground treated with quicklime to dissolve effluent. Few houses had running water or drains and it was a daily task to empty slops down open gullies in the streets.

HOMELESSNESS

Homelessness was a constant problem in towns, especially for those who were unable to work, who were literally put out onto the streets. Alcohol was cheap (beer was less than 1p per pint) and easier to acquire than good drinking water, so drunkenness was a problem, even amongst children.

STREET TRADERS

The streets offered numerous opportunities to earn a living. Traders sold their wares, such as bread, milk and pies, from hand carts. Girls might sell cut flowers while boys might offer fresh poultry or a shoe shine.

COMPARATIVE LIFESTYLES

These two views show the comparison between the poor and wealthy sectors of 19th century towns. The rich could afford elegant, well-built villas, while the poor had to tolerate the squalor of cramped, back-to-back housing surrounded by noise and filth.

LIFE FOR THE RICH

THE HIGH LIFE

For many wealthy young ladies life was an endless round of social gatherings, attending balls, the opera or the theatre, so as to be seen by prospective husbands.

*T*he Victorian age saw the emergence of a new tier of social class, wealthy businessmen who made vast fortunes from the new advances in technology, though often at the expense of the working classes who were forced to work in appalling conditions for low wages. Until the rise of the Victorian industrial entrepreneurs, most of the country's wealth lay in land ownership, particularly the estates of the aristocracy, but now any enterprising individual could become rich.

A STITCH IN TIME

New technology and mass-production brought many labour-saving devices, including the sewing machine, invented in 1851 by Singer. This sewing machine, manufactured by Wheeler and Wilson, is considered to be the forerunner of the modern lock-stitch and revolutionised clothes manufacture.

QUEEN VICTORIA

- *Born 1819*
- *Ascended the throne 1837*
- *Died 1901*

Victoria was proud of the technical achievements of her reign and allowed many new devices to be used in the royal household, such as electric lighting and carpet cleaners.

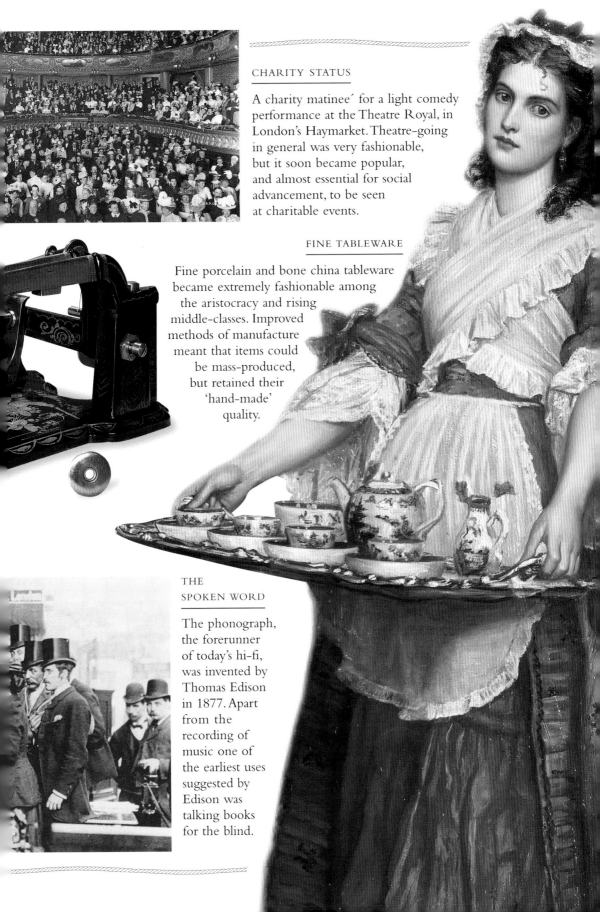

CHARITY STATUS

A charity matinee´ for a light comedy
performance at the Theatre Royal, in
London's Haymarket. Theatre-going
in general was very fashionable,
but it soon became popular,
and almost essential for social
advancement, to be seen
at charitable events.

FINE TABLEWARE

Fine porcelain and bone china tableware
became extremely fashionable among
the aristocracy and rising
middle-classes. Improved
methods of manufacture
meant that items could
be mass-produced,
but retained their
'hand-made'
quality.

THE SPOKEN WORD

The phonograph,
the forerunner
of today's hi-fi,
was invented by
Thomas Edison
in 1877. Apart
from the
recording of
music one of
the earliest uses
suggested by
Edison was
talking books
for the blind.

THE POOR AT HOME

*A*lthough the technological revolution brought wealth to industrialists, it brought abject poverty to the working classes. Many were forced to work long hours, under appalling conditions, for low wages. Many chose to emigrate to Australia, America and Canada. One way out of the poverty trap was to work in service in the houses of the wealthy. There were over one million domestic servants in 1851 out of a population of just 20 million.

DESTITUTION

Many of the homeless lived in workhouses where, in payment for working during the day, they received a meal and a bed. This old woman was so destitute that she could not work and slept on the steps of the workhouse. She minded a friend's baby in return for food.

CHILDREN'S HOMES

Homelessness was an ever-growing problem in towns, particularly among children, whose parents might have died. Dr. Thomas Barnado opened his first home for poor boys (many of whom had run away to escape the cruelty of factory conditions) in London in 1870, providing them with food and shelter.

PAWNBROKERS

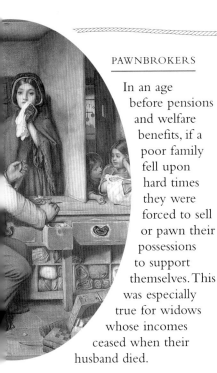

In an age before pensions and welfare benefits, if a poor family fell upon hard times they were forced to sell or pawn their possessions to support themselves. This was especially true for widows whose incomes ceased when their husband died.

LEARNING BY ROTE

Few working class children received any education because it was felt it would make them discontent with their lot. The fortunate few went to dame schools, charitable institutions run by women in their own homes, where reading, writing and simple arithmetic were taught.

COTTAGE INDUSTRIES

It was not uncommon for poor couples to have as many as 9 or 10 children. Although this view shows a typical family with the children at play (probably on a Sunday, the only day of rest) the whole family was expected to work. Even those children not sent out to work in factories and mills had to help support the family by doing chores around the house or making items for sale.

FOOD & DRINK

One of the biggest problems facing Victorian society was how to feed a population that was growing at an alarming rate. In pre-industrial Britain, the majority of people worked on the land and produced their own food. Most people now worked in factories and had to buy all their food with their wages, marking the beginnings of the modern consumer society.

DELIVERED TO YOUR DOOR

Milk was delivered straight from the farm. Customers took their jugs out into the street to the milkman, who filled them from large churns.

SPOILT FOR CHOICE

Never before had such a range of foods been available as cheap imports flooded in from abroad. Even the meagre diets of the poor gradually improved and became more varied. Such items as tea, for long an expensive luxury, became affordable by all.

CONVENIENCE FOODS

One of the solutions to keeping food fresh was this dry-air syphon refrigerator (c.1900). Food was chilled by the insulation of ice blocks in an adjoining compartment, which circulated cold air. Towards the end of the Victorian era tinned foods also became available.

HOME DELIVERIES

In smaller towns, and in villages, street tradesmen still carried their wares from door-to-door. Fresh bread, fish, dairy products and vegetables were often sold this way, but in larger towns, especially towards the end of the 19th century, improved standards of hygiene meant that more and more people bought their food from shops, where it was better protected.

THE MIDDLE MAN

Markets are a survival from the pre-industrialised age, when few shops existed and buyers and sellers met to exchange goods. At town wholesale markets, like Covent Garden fruit and vegetable market in London, shown here, larger traders bought goods in bulk from several suppliers at cheaper prices, which they then sold on to smaller traders for a profit.

PASTIMES

Cricket, first played in the 16th century, grew in popularity and became a gentleman's pursuit. W.G. Grace, perhaps the most famous cricketer of all time, lifted the game to its present status. He had an active playing career of 35 years and on one occasion amassed the score of 224 not out.

For most people Sunday was the only day when they did not have to work, so many simply rested. For others, cheap railway transport meant that for the first time they could visit other areas. Day trips to seaside towns became popular, as did visits to the growing number of public art galleries and museums.

CHILDREN'S ENTERTAINMENT

Children in rural areas were sometimes treated to a performance by a travelling puppeteer with his 'Punch and Judy' show, a survival from medieval fairs.

THE NOUVEAU RICH

The wealth generated by industry created a new breed of entrepreneurs who amassed large, disposable incomes. Gambling had always been popular, but exclusive casinos and gentlemen's clubs were established in an attempt to legitimise the pursuit.

Every town could boast at least one, in many cases several, theatres and music halls, showing everything from variety shows to plays, opera and ballet. In the 1890s over 350 music halls opened in London alone.

THE DAY OF SETTLEMENT

These characters are settling their debts at the Derby. Gambling on sporting events has always been popular, but never more so than in Victorian times. It was one of the rare occasions when people from different backgrounds mixed socially.

TRADITIONAL SKILLS

Traditional needlework and embroidery skills remained the main pastime for many middle and upper class ladies. This design has been used for the title page of a children's book on dolls' houses, the manufacture of which became extremely popular in Victorian times.

BESIDE THE SEASIDE

Although the benefits of sea bathing had been discovered in the 18th century, it was the coming of the railway age that made seaside excursions possible for the masses.

FASHION

As is the case in all ages, clear distinctions were drawn between the fashions worn by people from different social backgrounds. The poor invariably wore clothes that were practical, giving few concessions to fashion, while the rich could afford better materials and indulge themselves in more elaborate styles, purely for the look, even though many were extremely uncomfortable to wear. People from all classes tended to keep a special set of clothes for Sunday best.

A FULLER FIGURE

By about 1870 bustles replaced crinoline. Skirts were draped over a frame of padded cushions to give more fullness to the back of the dress.

FASHION CONSCIOUSNESS

Narrow waists were very fashionable for ladies, right up to the end of Victoria's reign. This was achieved by wearing corsets made of steel, wood or bone, which were so tightly laced that they restricted breathing, causing some women to faint.

FASHION ACCESSORIES

Ladies carried many fashion accessories, particularly when attending social functions. In addition to jewellery, they might carry a fan, such as the one shown here, complete with artificial flower decoration. Hair styles were more elaborate, often incorporating wigs and false hair pieces. Gentlemen usually carried gloves and a walking cane.

FOLLOWERS OF FASHION

Working class children wore cast-offs or cut-down adult clothes, while wealthier families dressed their children very formally in miniature versions of adult styles. Boys and girls both wore dresses until about five years old.

CHANGING FACE OF FASHION

The invention of the sewing machine did not make seamstresses, tailors and shoemakers redundant (in 1891 over a quarter of a million people worked in clothes manufacture) but instead made more elaborate designs possible. Ladies' shoes in particular became far more daring in their design as a result of mechanisation. Gentlemen wore spats, short cloth gaiters below their trouser bottoms to protect their shoes from mud.

COSTUME JEWELLERY

Many precious and semi-precious stones were imported from the east, particularly from India, where they were quite common, and used to decorate items of fashion jewellery.

ART &
ARCHITECTURE

*V*ictorian art and architecture was often dismissed as contributing nothing new and original. While they did produce the Gothic and Classical revivals, the development of graceful structures, such as bridges and canopies using iron, steel and glass are wholly their own. Literary giants like Charles Dickens, Sir Walter Scott and the Brontë sisters developed the novel to its full potential, while probably the most original group of English painters, the Pre-Raphaelites, emerged during this time when Millais, Rossetti, Hunt and other like-minded artists formed a school of art that reflected the spirit of the age.

SPOKESMAN FOR THE AGE

Charles Dickens (1812-70) was the greatest and most popular novelist of his day. His graphic descriptions of Victorian England give us a good idea of what life was really like, particularly for the poor. All of his books were serialised, making them available to all classes.

THE CRYSTAL PALACE

The Great Exhibition of 1851 was the brainchild of Prince Albert and was housed in the purpose-built Crystal Palace. It was a masterpiece of cast iron and glass, designed by Joseph Paxton, covering 26 acres and measuring three times the length of St. Paul's Cathedral. Incredibly, the building survived a move from Hyde Park to Sydenham after the exhibition, but sadly burned down in 1936.

Many art galleries and museums opened in towns throughout Britain to educate the masses and introduce ordinary people to the wider world of art.

TRAGIC GENIUS

The Brontë sisters, Anne, Emily and Charlotte, all wrote under male pseudonyms to improve their chances of success. They lived in lonely isolation on the Yorkshire moors and died within seven years of one another, all at young ages.

HEALTH & MEDICINE

The main health problem facing Victorians, particularly in the towns, was that of overcrowding and the public health problems associated with it. The large numbers of people living in the densely packed slum houses produced a lot of waste, but there was no proper means to dispose of it. Streets became open sewers which led to many outbreaks of diseases such as typhoid and cholera. A series of Public Health Acts from 1848 on were passed in Parliament making it the responsibility of local councils to provide drainage and clean water supplies and clear away slums.

MEDIEVAL CURES

Prior to the discovery in around 1856 by such scientists as Louis Pasteur that disease was caused by microscopic bacteria, medical knowledge had advanced little since the middle ages. Crude treatments, like blood–letting to remove toxins, were still widely practiced.

THE WATER CLOSET

As sewerage systems improved so flushable toilets became more common in rich households. The poor usually shared a communal 'earth closet' outside, which was often relocated as the cesspit beneath it filled with effluent.

SHOCK TACTICS

In 1867 Joseph Lister developed an antiseptic to kill bacteria, which increased the survival rate from surgery dramatically. Prior to that over half of patients died from shock, gangrene or secondary infections.

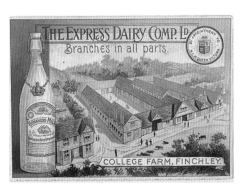

POOR DIET

Many children, deprived of sunlight and clean air, and fed a poor, unbalanced diet, developed rickets, a debilitating disease causing bone malformation. Fresh milk containing plenty of vitamin D helped reduce the incidence of the disease.

WATERBORNE DISEASES

Following numerous outbreaks of typhoid and cholera in overcrowded towns, a link was discovered by Edwin Chadwick between disease and poor living conditions. Massive sewers were constructed to improve the drainage and carry dirty water out to sea.

DENTAL HYGIENE

This Victorian dentist's surgery shows treadle-operated drills. The successful use of chloroform as an anaesthetic after 1847 made it possible to remove teeth or perform operations painlessly.

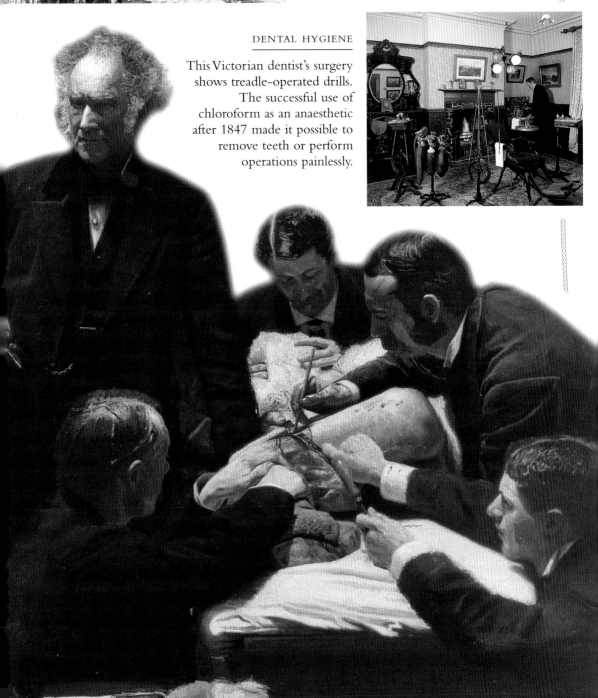

LOVE & MARRIAGE

Women from all classes were expected to marry young (usually about age 18) and to raise a family and so were not considered eligible for a career. Upper and middle class girls were usually chaperoned when meeting young men. If a woman had a child out of wedlock she was scorned by society and might become a social outcast, forced to enter a workhouse in order to survive.

ARRANGED MARRIAGES

Few marriages were love matches, but were arranged by parents who chose a suitable spouse for their children.

OFF TO THE WARS

With so many servicemen deployed around the Empire, many wives were forced to bring up the family single-handed. This picture shows a wife saying farewell to her husband on the eve of his embarkation.

WILD OATS

Young men from wealthy families were often expected to gain sexual experience from liaisons with women of a lower social order, but marriage between people from different classes was frowned upon and might lead to disinheritance from the family estate.

A SPINSTER'S LIFE

Unmarried women were regarded as the property of their fathers, who could also claim any wages they earned. Most parents, however, wanted to see their children married off, particularly daughters, who might have no means of support should anything happen to their fathers.

ROYAL PROPOSAL

According to the dictates of royal protocol, no man is allowed to propose to a queen, so Victoria had to ask for Albert's hand in marriage, unusual for the day. She is seen here surrounded by her children and grandchildren.

WOMEN & CHILDREN

LIFE OF EASE

While boys from wealthy families were groomed for a profession, girls were not expected to work. They spent much of their time entertaining or making social calls to friends and neighbours.

*L*ife for women and children in the 19th century was unbearably hard and few born to poverty had the opportunity to better themselves. Social reformers, like Lord Shaftesbury, did much to improve things and a series of Acts were passed in the 1840s reducing working hours to 10 a day and improving conditions, but unscrupulous employers continued to exploit their workforce.

COMPULSORY EDUCATION

In 1870 the government passed an Education Act stating that all children between the ages of 5-10 must attend school. The education was not free and many poorer families could not afford to send their children. After 1891 schooling became free to all.

Women of all classes were regarded as the property of their husbands, as were any wages they earned. Until the Property Act of 1882 all of a woman's property automatically belonged to her husband.

IMPRISONED BY CIRCUMSTANCE

Many women were forced to take their children to prison with them if convicted of a crime, rather than abandon them. Prison reformer Elizabeth Fry helped to improve the often squalid conditions inside and set up schools for the children.

PRISONERS IN THEIR OWN HOMES

The years of innocence in Victorian childhood were short-lived. Children were considered the property of their father, who could send them out to work as young as five years old and keep all their wages to help support the family. Children could be imprisoned in their own homes, a right husbands had even over their wives until 1891.

WOMEN'S EQUALITY?

Women had few rights in 19th century Britain and had to perform the same tasks as men at work, but for much less pay. These ladies were photographed at an iron foundry in South Wales in 1865.

WAR & WEAPONRY

*S*till basking in the reflected glory of Waterloo, the British were unprepared for the harsh realities of the Crimean War with Russia (1854–56). Afterwards Britain concentrated its military efforts on either extending or defending the realms of the Empire, which covered one quarter of the world's land mass, the largest empire ever known.

HONOURABLE DISCHARGE

Methods of warfare changed drastically during the 19th century as new technology developed more efficient weapons, such as this rapid-firing gatling gun of 1870. Mechanisation had the effect of dehumanising warfare which, until then, had always been considered an honourable pursuit.

EMPIRE BUILDING

With increased poverty and unemployment at home, there was no shortage of volunteers to sign up for the many military campaigns of Victoria's empire-building reign; better to risk your life and die with honour than to die destitute.

THE INDIAN MUTINY

Since the 18th century the East India Company had administered India, with help from the army, supplemented by Indian troops. In 1857 the native troops, supported by many Indian princes, rebelled against British rule. The rebellion was crushed and afterwards India was placed under direct rule of the British government.

GUERRILLA WARFARE

In 1899 war broke out in South Africa between Dutch settlers, the Boers, and the British. A massive army was sent to crush them, but it proved ineffective against the Boers' guerrilla tactics. Scarcely a victory for the British, peace was eventually achieved in 1902.

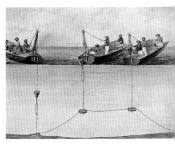

DETERRENT

Alfred Nobel, a Swedish scientist, invented dynamite and other explosive substances, for use in civil engineering projects and as a deterrent to promote world peace. However, military authorities, including Britain, used them to make weapons, such as these sea mines used to blow up ships.

VALLEY OF DEATH

The 'Charge of the Light Brigade' at Balaclava in the Crimea in 1854, was one of Britain's worst military disasters. Confused orders and incompetent officers culminated in a futile charge straight towards the massed Russian guns. Nearly half of the 673 cavalrymen died or were wounded.

STREET CRIME

Gangs of thieves roamed the dingy streets of Victorian towns at night and often garroted their victims.

CRIME & PUNISHMENT

*W*ith so much poverty and such appalling living conditions, many people turned to crime as a way of life. Punishments were severe, even for children, who might be imprisoned for stealing a loaf of bread. Prisons were so overcrowded that 'hulks' were moored in river estuaries to house the overspill. Many convicts were sent to the colonies to serve out their sentences.

INDECENT ASSAULT

Victorians were sensitive to moral standards; this music hall dancer was imprisoned for three months on the grounds of indecency for wearing this costume in public.

ROYAL SCAPEGOAT

Many people blamed Victoria herself for their hardships and several attempts were made on her life. This attempt was by an out-of-work Irishman in 1849.

DEATH PENALTY

At the beginning of the 19th century over 200 crimes were punishable by death. Despite reforms, there were still over 70 crimes carrying the death sentence in Victorian times, including petty theft and assault.

WHEEL OF MISFORTUNE

Conditions inside Victorian prisons were cramped and primitive. Treadmills, similar to the one shown here, were used as a form of exercise or to punish unruly prisoners.

A POLICEMAN'S LOT

Until the reform bills of Sir Robert Peel in the 1820s, when a proper civilian police force was set up in London, many criminals got away unpunished. By early Victorian times most towns had their own police force to apprehend villains, often recruited from the armed services and run along similar lines.

TRANSPORT & SCIENCE

IMPROVED ROADS

SMILE!

Cameras, first developed in the 19th century, were for the first time in history able to record events as they happened, though initially they were used as reconnaissance aids by the military.

*B*ritain's scientists and engineers led the world with their array of technological inventions, such as the development of steam and internal combustion engines, electricity and building techniques. Many of the familiar household objects today, such as light bulbs, typewriters, packaged food and hi-fi had their origins in the Victorian age. Britain became known as the 'workshop of the world'.

The first motor cars (invented c.1865) resembled horseless carriages and were open to the elements. They needed metalled surfaces to run effectively, which led to road improvements with the development of tarmacadamed surfaces.

UNDERWATER TACTICS

The development of the submarine and self-propelled torpedoes in both Britain and France changed the face of modern warfare. The one shown here, invented by the Rev. G. W. Garret in 1880 was launched on rails.

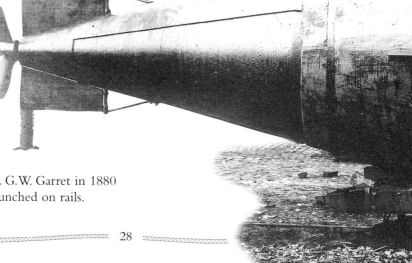

ON THE RIGHT TRACK

The Victorian age saw the rapid development of railways. For the first time in history fast, cheap transport was available to the masses, giving greater mobility to the population. Between 1829 and 1900, 22,000 miles of track were laid in Britain and in 1863 the world's first underground railway was opened in London.

MASS-PRODUCTION

Advancements in technology made it possible to mass-produce economically all manner of items for everyday use that previously had to be individually hand-made at great expense, such as this practical tape measure.

IT'S GOOD TO TALK

The telephone was invented by Alexander Graham Bell in 1875. Although greeted with enthusiasm, it was very expensive to install and initially only available to the rich. It was not possible to dial to another user directly. Connection had to be through an operator. Businessmen, who could better afford them, saw the potential of telephones and benefited enormously from improved communication links.

RELIGION

To most Christians, up to Victorian times, the Bible was taken as literal truth and few people questioned its authenticity. When Charles Darwin and others challenged this view with their revolutionary theories of evolution by natural selection, they shattered the beliefs of ordinary people and clergy alike. Many were unable to reconcile their religious feelings with the new scientific theories and Darwin suffered open derision from the public throughout his life.

CHALLENGE TO THE CHURCH

The biologist Charles Huxley championed Darwin's theories of evolution when the church attacked his views and tried to discredit him as a heretic.

SUNDAY SCHOOLS

For many working class children, who worked all week, Sunday or charity schools, organised by the church, were the only form of education they received. Apart from learning to read, the only other subject usually taught was Bible studies.

A religious fervour and strict moral upbringing swept Victorian society, particularly the upper and middle classes. For the first time since the Reformation many new churches were built, or medieval ones restored. At the beginning of Victoria's reign (1837) about 60% of the population regularly went to church on Sundays; today the figure is less than 1%.

THE DESCENT OF MAN

When Charles Darwin published 'The Origin of the Species' in 1859 he caused a furore by challenging the biblical account of the Creation, in which God created man in his own likeness. According to Darwin, man evolved gradually from an ape-like creature over many thousands of years.

THE 'SALLY ARMY'

The self-styled 'General' William Booth founded the Salvation Army in 1878. Originally a Methodist preacher, he modelled his church along army lines to combat intemperance, prostitution and exploitation of the working classes. He also helped rehabilitate discharged prisoners and introduced legal aid for the poor.

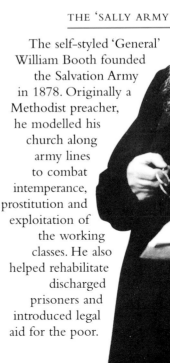

THE OXFORD MOVEMENT

Evangelicalism had its origins in Oxford. A group of like-minded men felt that the Anglican Church had become lax in its duties towards the poor and so formed a new church with a more humanitarian doctrine.

A GLOSSARY OF INTERESTING TERMS

Char - A word introduced into the English language from the days when the British Empire extended into much of Asia. Now a slang work for a cup of tea, it comes from the chinese word for tea, cha.

Co-operative - The chain of modern stores known as co-operatives (or co-ops) had their origins in Lancashire in 1844, when a group of weavers, co-operating with one another, opened a grocery store that shared its profits with their customers in the form of a dividend.

Dickensian - A term originally applied to the characters of Charles Dickens novels, but now used to describe anything of a primitive or poor quality, particularly in relation to social conditions.

Jodhpurs - these close-fitting trousers, still used when riding horses today, were first introduced in Victorian times from Jodhpur, in India, where they formed part of the traditional dress.

Pasteurised - the treatment known as pasteurisation to kill germs in food and drink takes its name from the French scientist Louis Pasteur, who discovered the link between bacteria and disease in 1856.

Strike - In 1888 women working in a London match factory withdrew their labour to get better working conditions. The word strike (from striking a match) is now used to describe similar industrial actions.

Victoria Cross - the highest military decoration for conspicuous bravery was first instituted by Victoria herself in 1856.

ACKNOWLEDGEMENTS

We would like to thank: Graham Rich, Tracey Pennington, Liz Rowe and Peter Done for their assistance. Copyright (c) 1997 *ticktock* Publishing Ltd.

First published in Great Britain by *ticktock* Publishing Ltd, Century Place, Lamberts Road, Tunbridge Wells, Kent, TN2 3EH. All rights reserved. No part of this publication may be reproduced, stored in a retrieval system, or transmitted in any form or by any means, electronic, mechanical, photocopying, recording or otherwise, without prior written permission of the copyright owner.

Printed in Hong Kong

Acknowledgements: Picture Credits t=top, b=bottom, l=left, OFC=outside front cover, IFC=inside front cover, IBC=inside back cover, OBC=outside front cover. ·

The Games Room 1889, Jean Beraud (c) ADAGP, Paris and DACS, London 1997 (Musee Carnavalet, Paris/Giraudon/Bridgeman Art Library, London); 12/13b. By courtesy of BT Archives; 29cr & OBC. B.T. Batsford Ltd; 6/7b. Barnado's Photographic Archive (D58); 8bl & OBC. The Beamish. The North of England Open Air Museum; 19cr. Bodleian Library, University of Oxford: John Johnson Collection; Political General folder 1; 4l, 5br & 32, Trades of Professions 6; 4/5b, Educational 16; 9tr, Trade in Prints and Scraps 9, 13cl, Trade in Prints and Scraps 7, 18l & OBC, Food 2; 18cb, Alphabets3; 30/31t. Sheffield City Art Galleries/Bridgeman Art Library, London; OFCc. FORBES Magazine Collection, New York/Bridgeman Art Library, London; 6bl & OBC, 21cr, 31tr. Christopher Wood Gallery, London/Bridgeman Art Library, London; 9tl; 12/13b. Marylebone Cricket Club, London/Bridgeman Art Library, London; 12l & OFC. Jefferson College Philadelphia/Bridgeman Art Library, London; 19b. Guildhall Art Gallery, Corporation of London/Bridgemean Art Library, London; 20b. Mary Evans Picture Library; 3tl, 3tr, 3c, 5tl, 5tr, 12cr, 13cr, 16tl & OBC, 22/23c, 23tr & OFC, 23cr, 24l & OFC, 24/25 & OBC, 25t, 25cr, 26tl, 26/27b & OBC, 27tr & OBC, 28r & OFC. By courtesy of Fine Art Photographic Library; 15tr, 16/17b, 17t, 20tl, 25c, 25b, 29t, 30b. Galerie Berko/Fine Art Photographic Library; 8/9b, 11t. Haynes Fine Art/Fine Art Photographic Library; 6t. Hollywood Road Gallery/Fine Art Photographic Library; 14bl. N.R. Omell Gallery/Fine Art Photographic Library; 7r. Polak Gallery/Fine Art Photographic Library; 13t, 22tl, 22bl. Sutcliffe Galleries/Fine Art/Photographic Library; 3br, 21tl. Guildhall Library, Corporation of London; 5c, 10br. From the John Hillelson Collection; 8tl, 26cr. Hulton Getty; 2l, 7tl, 14tl, 19tl, 21br, 27cl, 30tl. Hunting Aerofims Lty (Mills 147); 13br & OFC. The Illustrated London News Picture Library; 27tl. Museum of London; IFC/1, 14/15t, 14/15b & OFC, 15br. By courtesy of the National Portrait Gallery, London 17cr. Oxfordshire Photographic Archive, DLA, OCC; 2r, 10l, 31bl. Popperfoto; 23br. Rural History Centre, University of Reading; 11cb. The Salvation Army International Heritage Centre; 31br. Science Museum/Science & Society Picture Library; 6/7c & OBC, 11cl, 18tr, 28tl & OFC, 28/29b, 29c.

Every effort has been made to trace the copyright holders and we apologise in advance for any unintentional omissions. We would be pleased to insert the appropriate acknowledgement in any subsequen edition of this publication.

A CIP Catalogue record for this book is available from the British Library. ISBN 1 86007 005 1

snapping-turtle guide

THE WRITER & HIS TIMES

harles Dickens's birth in 1812 came at a turbulent time in British history. King George III was on the throne, but his mental instability meant that his son, George, Prince of Wales, effectively ruled as Prince Regent. The country was nearing the end of 20 years of war with France – Napoleon was finally defeated at the Battle of Waterloo in 1815. Finally, the Industrial Revolution was changing the way that people in Britain both worked and lived. Not everyone liked these changes. In the year of Dickens's birth there were 'Luddite' riots. Workers broke into factories and smashed the new machinery which, they claimed, would put them out of work.

THE INDUSTRIAL REVOLUTION

Britain was the first country in the world to undergo the changes that became known as the Industrial Revolution. Starting in the late 18th century, small-scale production in workshops began to be replaced by large-scale manufacturing in mills and factories using spinning machines like the one above. New inventions speeded up manufacturing processes, and coal pits were opened up to provide the fuel needed to power the new machinery.

VICTORIAN TOURISTS

The speed with which railways were built across Britain during the middle of the 19th century was amazing. Rail transport was much faster and much cheaper than anything before it; for the first time, many ordinary people could afford to travel. In 1841, Thomas Cook organized his first railway excursion, which went from Leicester to Loughborough. Cook's tours soon became highly popular – this cartoon pokes fun at the people who went on them.

STEPHENSON'S *ROCKET*

The Industrial Revolution also led to a revolution in methods of transport. A major breakthrough came with the development of steam engines that moved on metal tracks. In 1825, a railway was opened between Stockton and Darlington in northern England, proving that rail transport could be both efficient and cheap. George Stephenson, who built this railway, had another success in 1829 with his locomotive, *Rocket*, at the Rainhill locomotive trials. A year later, the world's first passenger railway opened between Liverpool and Manchester.

GREAT EXHIBITION, 1851

In 1851, the Great Exhibition was held in Hyde Park in London. It was the idea of Queen Victoria's husband, Prince Albert, to celebrate the *'Works of Industry of all Nations'*. However, it also showed that Britain led the world in all areas of industry. A huge building, made from glass, was erected especially for the occasion and named the Crystal Palace. Dickens visited the Great Exhibition but did not like it much, saying that *'so many things bewildered me . . .'*

TURBULENT TIMES

In 1839, there was a riot at Newport in Monmouthshire, which ended in death and bloodshed when the military was called in to deal with the protesters. As tempers flared, guns were fired. This was one of the Chartist riots, which marked the years 1838–42. The Chartists took their name from 'The People's Charter', which was drawn up in 1838. Their demands included the right to vote for all men, annual general elections and the right to vote in secret. Chartist petitions were rejected twice by parliament and the movement fizzled out, but some of their reforms were introduced later in the century.

CRIME & PUNISHMENT

Crime and the harsh punishments meted out by Victorian society in response to it, coloured much of Dickens's writings. The family's spell in Marshalsea prison left a mark on Dickens, but even more influential was the prison at Newgate. Newgate was also a place of public execution, where crowds would gather to watch the guilty make their appointment with the hangman's noose. Dickens was repelled yet at the same time fascinated by such brutality. In *Oliver Twist*, Oliver witnesses Fagin in the cells before he is hung at Newgate, while Hugh, Dennis and Barnaby are imprisoned in the institution in *Barnaby Rudge*. The idea of falling on the wrong side of the law, or having a criminal in the family is absolutely central to books such as *David Copperfield* and *Barnaby Rudge*.

HOMES ABROAD

The expansion of the transport network meant that Dickens was able to travel abroad, which he did frequently. He stayed in Lausanne, Switzerland, and climbed Mount Vesuvius (above), where the dramatic scenery left a lasting impression on him. He also visited Paris, and the contrast between the French capital and London installed in him 'a ghostly idea' that was to find expression in *A Tale of Two Cities*.

CLASS & SOCIETY

As Dickens's fame and wealth increased, he and his family moved to increasingly fashionable addresses in London. But although he was a member of polite London society, Dickens was no stranger to the other side of London – the areas of poverty and misery that he knew only too well from his childhood. Even as a prosperous author, Dickens remained both fascinated and appalled by the poor areas of London, and he would often walk the streets of the city at night, observing and thinking. In his novels, he tried to address some of the injustices that he saw around him by bringing them to the attention of the wider reading public in an imaginative form. Many of those injustices were brought about as a result of the oppressive nature of the institutions of Victorian England, such as the law, petty government bureaucracy and the workhouse.

THE WORLD OF CHARLES DICKENS

Charles Dickens was born in Portsmouth, but spent much of his childhood in Kent, before his family moved to London in 1822. Dickens came to know London intimately, and the city provides the backdrop for many of his novels. Dickens also travelled widely in Europe, and made two visits to North America, and one of his novels, *Martin Chuzzlewit*, is set in America. Wherever he went, Dickens was a keen observer of all human life, from the poorest to the wealthiest in 19th-century society. It was this keen eye, as well as a vivid imagination and a sense of the comic that inspired much of his writing.

THE WORLD OF THE THEATRE

From an early age, Dickens was intrigued by the theatre. He saw productions at the Covent Garden Theatre and Drury Lane in London, and also at the local Theatre Royal in Rochester (above). He also visited 'private theatres', where anyone could walk the boards for a small fee. Dickens delighted in not only the plays themselves, but also the often poor quality of the acting. This influenced his writing, where his comedy centred around the difference between life's ideals and the rather different realities.

EARLY READING

Dickens was heavily influenced by writers such as Henry Fielding, but equally by folk tales and legends such as Little Red Riding Hood. Dickens wrote that *'Little Red Riding Hood was my first love. I felt that if I could have married her, I should have known perfect bliss.'* The directness of the storytelling, the 'larger than life' characters and the powerful flights of imagination characterize much of his writing.

DICKENS'S CONTEMPORARIES

ickens had a wide circle of friends, including many of the most prominent writers, artists, actors and politicians of the day. Dickens also met some notable literary figures on his travels, including Edgar Allan Poe and Henry Wadsworth Longfellow. One of Dickens's greatest admirers, the Danish writer Hans Christian Andersen, was thrilled to be invited to visit Gad's Hill. Unfortunately, Andersen outstayed his welcome, prompting Dickens to write on a card: *'Hans Christian Andersen slept in this room for five weeks, which seemed to the family ages!'*

WILLIAM THACKERAY (1811–63)

William Thackeray is best known for his novel *Vanity Fair*, published in 1847. Dickens and Thackeray were friendly and praised each other's work, but there seems to have been some rivalry or unease between the two authors. This came to a head in a quarrel in 1858, the same year that Dickens left his wife, Catherine, to whom Thackeray was sympathetic.

The estrangement between the two men lasted until shortly before Thackeray's death in 1863. At Thackeray's funeral, Dickens was described as having *'a look of bereavement on his face which was indescribable'*.

WILKIE COLLINS (1824–89)

Wilkie Collins is best remembered today as the author of *The Moonstone* and *The Woman in White*. This illustration shows him pasting up a poster for the latter. He contributed to Dickens's weekly periodicals, *Household Words* and *All The Year Round*, and worked with Dickens on a number of short stories. Collins's brother, Charles, married Dickens's daughter, Kate, in 1860. However, Dickens disapproved of the match because Charles Collins suffered from poor health.

ALFRED LORD TENNYSON (1809-92)

This image appeared on the cover of Tennyson's *Idylls of the King*, a series of verses on the legends of King Arthur, in 1875. Dickens knew and admired Tennyson's poetry. We know that he read *Idylls of the King* during the same summer that he was busy writing *A Tale of Two Cities*, in 1859. Tennyson visited the Dickens family when they were living in Switzerland, not long after Dickens had christened his sixth child Alfred d'Orsay Tennyson Dickens in honour of the poet.

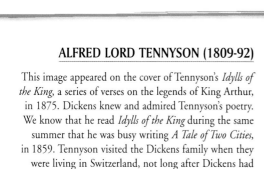

ANTHONY TROLLOPE (1815-82)

Anthony Trollope's father was a failed lawyer who died young, forcing his mother, Frances, to turn to writing in order to provide for her family. Trollope followed in her footsteps, having his first real success with *The Warden*, published in 1855. This was the first in a series, known as the Barchester Novels. In *The Warden*, Trollope based the character of the editor of *The Jupiter* on Dickens. Trollope later referred to Dickens as '*Mr Popular Sentiment*'.

GEORGE ELIOT (1819–80)

George Eliot was the pen-name used by Mary Ann Evans, one of the greatest of the Victorian novelists and much admired by Dickens. She and Dickens met several times. After he read her novel, *Adam Bede*, he wrote: '*The conception of Hetty's character is so extraordinarily subtle and true, that I laid the book down fifty times, to shut my eyes and think about it.*' Dickens tried to persuade Eliot to write a story for publication in *All The Year Round*, but was unsuccessful.

JOHN & ELIZABETH DICKENS

When Dickens was born, his father John was working in the Naval Pay Office at the dockyard in Portsmouth. His mother, Elizabeth, was just 23. They had married in 1809 in the church of St. Mary-le-Strand, and this entry from the marriage register records the event. Elizabeth had another six children over the next 15 years, two of whom died in infancy. John Dickens was an easy-going and hospitable man, who was incapable of living within his means and was always in debt. More than once the family was forced to move house – either because he could not pay the rent or to escape angry creditors.

DICKENS'S BIRTHPLACE

Dickens was born in this house on the outskirts of Portsmouth. The family did not stay here for very long after his birth. Five months later they were on the move, the first of many upheavals that marked Dickens's childhood. The house still stands today, and is open to the public.

TIMELINE

1812
Birth of Charles John Huffam Dickens.

1817
Dickens family move to Chatham, Kent.

1822
Dickens family move to London.

1824
Dickens sent to work in Warren's Blacking Factory; father arrested for debt and imprisoned.

1827
Dickens starts work as a solicitor's clerk.

LIFE IN CHATHAM

In 1817, when Dickens was five, the family moved to Chatham in Kent, a bustling naval town near to the cathedral town of Rochester. This was the most settled period of Dickens's childhood. In 1822, however, this happy period came to an end when John Dickens was transferred to a new job in London, and the family moved to a small, shabby house in Bayham Street in Camden Town.

THE WRITER'S LIFE

*T*hroughout Dickens's childhood, the family was constantly dogged by money problems. Consequently, Dickens was sent to work in a shabby factory when he was 12, an experience that was to haunt him for the rest of his life.

SIBLING RIVALRY

In London, the family's financial problems grew steadily worse. The only respite for John and Elizabeth Dickens was the musical success of Dickens's favourite sister, Fanny. At the age of 11, she was accepted as a boarder at the Royal Academy of Music in London (above). When Fanny left to begin her training as a pianist and singer, Dickens was left behind in the backstreets of London to survive as best he could.

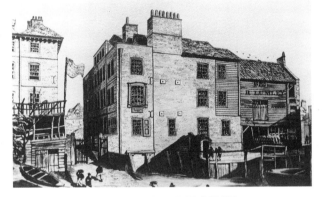

THE BLACKING FACTORY

As the family fell further and further into debt, the situation hit Dickens particularly hard. There was no money for him to go to school, but worse was to come. In 1824, John Dickens decided to accept an offer from a family relation for his son to work at Warren's Blacking factory at Hungerford Stairs in London (above). The job of 12-year-old Dickens was to cover the pots of boot blacking with paper and paste labels on to them. It was a time of utter misery for him. He later wrote of his feelings during this period: *'No words can express the secret agony of my soul.'*

FROM CHILD TO MAN

This portrait of the 18-year-old Dickens, painted by his aunt, Janet Barrow, is one of the earliest known. By the age of 18, he had already seen and experienced a great deal. While working in the blacking factory, his father was arrested for debt and the whole family, except for Charles and Fanny, were forced to move to Marshalsea debtor's prison. Dickens lived alone in lodgings in poverty. After a few months, a legacy released the family from prison and Dickens from the factory. In the following years he attended school and then became a solicitor's clerk. But he already had a different career in mind – journalism.

SKETCHES BY BOZ

After his first published article in 1833, Dickens continued to write sketches of London life for the *Monthly Magazine*. In August 1834, Dickens took up a post as a journalist on a newspaper called the *Morning Chronicle*. The editor of the paper encouraged him to carry on writing his sketches, which Dickens did under the name of 'Boz'. In 1836, a collection of these sketches, with illustrations by the well-known artist George Cruikshank, appeared under the name, *Sketches by Boz*. One of Cruikshank's illustrations for the book is shown here.

LONDON LIFE

During his years as a solicitor's clerk and a reporter, Dickens spent many hours walking around London. He came to know the city's streets and its inhabitants intimately. He began to put this detailed knowledge to good use by writing sketches of London life in all its variety. The first of these sketches to be accepted for publication appeared in the *Monthly Magazine* in 1833. This picture shows the young, hopeful Dickens posting his contribution into the editor's box.

TIMELINE

1830
Dickens meets Maria Beadnell.

1832
Dickens becomes a parliamentary shorthand reporter.

1833
Relationship with Maria Beadnell ends; first publication in Monthly Magazine.

1834
Dickens becomes a reporter for Morning Chronicle; meets Catherine Hogarth.

1836
Sketches published in Evening Chronicle.

1836
Sketches by Boz; Dickens and Catherine are married.

1837
The Pickwick Papers; son, Charles, born; Catherine's sister, Mary, dies suddenly.

1838
Oliver Twist; daughter, Mary (Mamie) is born.

1839
Daughter, Kate, born; Nicholas Nickleby.

FIRST LOVE

When he was 18, Dickens met Maria Beadnell (left), the daughter of a banker. He quickly fell deeply in love with her. However, her parents seem to have disapproved of the match – after all, no matter how ambitious Dickens was, he was still the son of a debtor. Dickens was eventually rejected by Maria. The episode affected him deeply, and he was later to draw on it to write the fictional account of David's love for Dora in his novel *David Copperfield*.

MARRIAGE & EARLY SUCCESS

*T*he 1830s were a significant time in Dickens's life. He fell in love for the first time, married and started a family, and his compositions began to be accepted for publication. His first published book was *Sketches by Boz*, which came out in 1836. At the same time, Dickens was already working on the monthly instalments of the book that really made his name, *The Pickwick Papers*. By the end of the decade he was a well-established and highly successful author.

THE HOGARTHS

The illustration above by Maclise shows Dickens with Catherine and Georgina Hogarth. Dickens met the Hogarth family in late 1834, after the journalist and music critic, George Hogarth, moved to London to work on the *Morning Chronicle*. Hogarth soon became editor of the *Evening Chronicle*, employing Dickens on his paper. Hogarth had a large family, and Dickens started to pay particular attention to his eldest daughter, Catherine (above middle). The two were soon engaged, although they did not marry for another year, in April 1836.

DICKENS'S PARLIAMENTARY CAREER

In 1827, Dickens left school and went to work as a solicitor's clerk. The work was deadly dull, and Dickens was determined to move on. He taught himself to write shorthand, mastering the dots, lines and squiggles in only a few months. By 1832, he had secured a position as a shorthand reporter in the original Houses of Parliament, which burned down soon after he left, and were replaced by the buildings on the left. His job was to note down parliamentary debates, and he soon had a reputation as one of the fastest and most accurate reporters ever seen in parliament.

A MOURNED FRIEND

This painting shows Catherine Hogarth's sister, Mary, who died at just 17 years of age in 1837. Dickens was very fond of Mary, describing her as 'a dear friend', and her death affected him deeply. Dickens experienced recurring dreams and visions of Mary 'sometimes as still living; sometimes as returning from the world of shadows to comfort me; always as being beautiful, placid and happy'. *The words Dickens wrote for her epitaph, where he described her as 'young, beautiful and good', occur several times in his books. Florence Dombey is described this way in* Dombey and Son, *while in* The Old Curiosity Shop, *Little Nell's death draws the same reaction.*

TRAVELS & FAME

ickens's endless energy meant that he was always working on several different projects, whether it be writing novels and plays or editing magazines. Sometimes his hectic schedule landed him in trouble when he could not fulfil his many obligations. Part of the pressure came from the fact that all of his novels were first published in instalments (mostly monthly, sometimes weekly), before being issued in book form. This method of publication brought his work to a wide audience. Soon every instalment of a new story by Dickens was keenly anticipated by an adoring public.

THE HEIRESS

In 1837, Angela Burdett-Coutts inherited a huge fortune from her grandfather, the banker Thomas Coutts. At about this time she met Charles Dickens, and she would consult him on how best to spend money on improving the lot of the poor (see page 27). She became a close family friend, even paying for Dickens's eldest son, Charley, to be educated at Eton. But when Dickens separated from Catherine, relations cooled between the two friends.

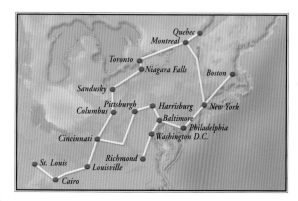

AMERICAN TRAVELS

Dickens's fame spread quickly beyond Britain and in January 1842, he and Catherine set off for a six-month tour of North America. Wherever they went, the streets were lined with onlookers wanting to catch a glimpse of the celebrity author, and invitations to dinners, receptions and balls poured in. Dickens and Catherine travelled to the West by train and paddleboat, and also visited the Niagara Falls in the north.

FAMILY LIFE

This portrait, painted in 1842 by Daniel Maclise shows the four eldest Dickens children: Charley, Mamie, Kate and Walter. Between 1837 and 1852, Catherine Dickens gave birth to ten children; three girls and seven boys. The youngest girl, Dora, was born in 1850 but died suddenly the following year. Dickens was distraught, particularly as his father had also recently died.

DICKENS AT WORK

Dickens's capacity for work was quite amazing. His publishers were constantly pressing him for a new novel, and he had many commitments as a journalist and editor. In addition, Dickens's frequent involvement in writing plays and theatrical productions placed further demands on his time. Many of the millions of words that poured from his imagination were written at this desk.

HOUSEHOLD WORDS

Despite his huge success as a novelist, Dickens cherished ambitions to run a newspaper or periodical – partly as a tool for reform, partly to raise extra income. After some unsuccessful ventures, he launched a weekly periodical called *Household Words* in 1850, which contained articles on a wide variety of subjects. It was a great success and sold up to 40,000 copies every week. Dickens's role on the front page was described as 'Conductor', but in fact he wrote large numbers of articles himself and carefully edited other contributions.

ACCIDENT AT STAPLEHURST

The strange double life led by both Dickens and Ellen Ternan meant that they often met abroad, away from prying eyes in England. Travelling back with Ellen's mother from a visit to France in 1865, the three were involved in a horrific train crash at Staplehurst in Kent. Many people were killed, but Dickens and the Ternans were able to crawl out of their carriage relatively unscathed. A fear of travelling by train haunted Dickens for the rest of his life.

LAST YEARS

In the last decade of his life, Dickens wrote *Great Expectations* and *Our Mutual Friend*. He also left an unfinished novel, *The Mystery of Edwin Drood*, when he died. Dickens died on 9 June, 1870 at Gad's Hill. He had asked to be buried in Rochester, but it was felt more appropriate that he should be buried in Westminster Abbey (see page 28).

LATER LIFE

*I*n 1857, Dickens met a young actress called Ellen Ternan, who was to become his companion for the remainder of his life. A year later, Dickens separated from Catherine. All the children except for the eldest, Charley, continued to live with their father. Catherine's sister, Georgina, who had been part of the Dickens household since 1842, also chose to stay with her brother-in-law, and was his housekeeper until his death. Despite ill-health, the final years of Dickens's life included another highly successful visit to America and public readings from his own works.

THE AUTHOR & THE ACTRESS

When Ellen Ternan met Dickens she was 18 years old – and he was 45. He quickly became infatuated with her, and the strength of his feelings became obvious when he ended his marriage to Catherine. He lost many friends as a result of this affair. Ellen met Dickens's children and frequently visited Gad's Hill, but both she and Dickens kept their relationship as secret as possible to avoid any scandal.

A DREAM HOME

As a boy growing up in Chatham, one of Dickens's favourite walks was past a large house called Gad's Hill Place. Dickens later remembered his father telling him that if he worked hard enough, this house could one day be his. In 1856, Dickens fulfilled his boyhood dream by buying Gad's Hill. He moved into it the following year, and it was his home until his death.

DRAMATIC READINGS

Dickens gave the first public reading of his work in 1853. This was the start of the reading tours that were to become a feature of the last part of Dickens's life, and people would flock to halls to witness the famous author reading excerpts from his short stories and novels. One of the most celebrated of these excerpts was Dickens's adaptation of the murder of Nancy from *Oliver Twist*. Fearing for the strain on his fragile health, family and friends urged him not to perform it. But Dickens was determined, and reported after one rendition that the audience were *'unmistakably pale, and had horror-stricken faces'*.

BOB CRATCHIT & TINY TIM

Bob Cratchit and Tiny Tim are two famous characters from Dickens's first, and best-known, 'Christmas book', *A Christmas Carol*. In this novel, the simple enjoyment of the poor Cratchit family is contrasted with the tight-fisted attitude of the miser, Ebenezer Scrooge. Dressed in threadbare clothes, with his crippled son to look after, the fate of Bob Cratchitt and his family is instrumental in Scrooge's eventual discovery of the true meaning of Christmas.

TONY WELLER

The appearance of Tony Weller in *The Pickwick Papers* ensured the success of the book. Samuel Pickwick meets Tony Weller at the White Hart Inn, Borough. He is described as wearing *'a coarse-striped waistcoat, with black calico sleeves and blue glass buttons; drab breeches and leggings. A bright red handkerchief was wound in a very loose and unstudied style round his neck.'*

LITTLE NELL

Nell Trent is the central figure in *The Old Curiosity Shop*. Her character is drawn partly from Dickens's sister-in-law, Mary (see page 11), who died suddenly in the author's arms not long after his marriage to Catherine. Dickens poured all his feelings into the fictional death of Little Nell, writing to the illustrator of the book *'I am breaking my heart over this story.'*

DICKENS'S CHARACTERS

ickens portrays all of Victorian society in his novels, from the aristocracy to the poorest of the working classes, and he was a keen observer of humanity. His books are full of larger-than-life characters, but Dickens was also fascinated by ordinary, middle-class people and their often rather shabby, mundane lives. In one of the *Sketches by Boz*, he wrote: *'It is strange with how little notice, good, bad or indifferent, a man may live and die in London. His existence is a matter of interest to no one save himself; he cannot be said to be forgotten when he dies, for no one remembered him when he was alive.'*

GHOSTLY PAINTING

This painting by Robert William Buss is titled *Dickens's Dream*. It shows Dickens surrounded by the ghostly outlines of characters and scenes from his books. After Dickens's death, G.H. Lewes, the partner of George Eliot, wrote: *'the joys and pains of childhood, the petty tyrannies of ignoble natures, the genial pleasantries of happy natures, the life of the poor, the struggles of the street and back parlour, the insolence of office, the sharp social contrasts, east-wind and Christmas jollity, hunger, misery and hot punch – these he could deal with so we laughed and cried'.*

BETSY TROTWOOD

David Copperfield's great-aunt, Betsy Trotwood, is one of the most endearing of all Dickens's characters. She has a sharp tongue and a heart of gold, and wages a daily battle against the donkeys that invade the lawn in front of her house. David notes *'To this hour I don't know whether my aunt had any lawful right of way over that patch of green; but she had settled it in her own mind that she had. The one great outrage of her life, demanding to be constantly avenged, was the passage of a donkey over that immaculate spot.'*

DICKENS AT HOME

Dickens's first proper home as a married man was at 48 Doughty Street (below), just west of Gray's Inn in London. He and Catherine moved there in April 1837. Their household also included Catherine's sister, Mary, and Dickens's brother Frederick. Today, 48 Doughty Street is home to the Dickens Museum. The Dickens family lived there until 1839, when they moved to a rather grander address, 1 Devonshire Terrace, in Regent's Park, (shown right).

CHILD POVERTY

Children suffered particularly badly in the slum districts of London. This beggar child was typical of the street urchins that roamed the streets of Victorian London. Dickens portrays neglected children in many of his novels, but probably the most famous of them all is Jo, the crossing-sweeper in *Bleak House*. This is how Dickens describes him: '*Dirty, ugly, disagreeable to all the senses. Homely filth begrimes him, homely parasites devour him, homely sores are in him, homely rags are on him.*'

DICKENS'S LONDON

'*Having been in London for two years, I thought I knew something of the town, but after a little talk with Dickens I found that I knew nothing. He knew it all from Bow to Brentford.*' These are the words of George Lear, a clerk who worked alongside the young Dickens in the office of the solicitors Ellis and Blackmore. As a child left alone to fend for himself, Dickens quickly got to know the streets and people of London. As an adult, he continued his explorations, often walking many miles at night revisiting old haunts and observing the life around him.

SEVEN DIALS

This engraving of the Seven Dials district of London was made by the French illustrator, Gustav Doré. Doré made many engravings showing the life of the poor in London. Dickens knew the Seven Dials area well. Nearby was St Giles, a slum district known as the 'rookery', where nearly 3,000 people lived in just 95 tumbledown houses without any sanitation. Not surprisingly, conditions in such places were appalling, and diseases such as cholera were an ever-present threat.

NEWGATE PRISON

As a small boy, Dickens often walked past the towering walls of Newgate Prison in London. It haunted his imagination, and appears in several of his works including *Sketches by Boz*, *The Old Curiosity Shop*, *Oliver Twist* and *Great Expectations*. In the historical novel *Barnaby Rudge*, Barnaby is imprisoned in Newgate but is freed when rioters break into the prison and release the prisoners. This novel was based on events in 1780, when the prison was burned down during anti-Catholic riots.

DICKENS & CHILDHOOD

Dickens never spoke about the painful events of his own childhood – particularly his time in the blacking factory – until a chance remark by his friend John Forster caused him to set down an account of his experiences. Dickens did not write an autobiography, but he did use his own childhood as inspiration for *David Copperfield*. Children appear as central characters in many of Dickens's other works, too, including *Great Expectations*, *Oliver Twist* and *Dombey and Son*.

COOLING CHURCHYARD

In the graveyard of Cooling church in Kent lie the lozenge-shaped graves of the children of the Comport family – 13 in all. None had lived beyond 17 months. Dickens often visited this wild and desolate place on the Kent marshes after he moved to Gad's Hill. It provided him with the inspiration for one of his most terrifying scenes, the encounter between Pip and the escaped convict Magwitch in *Great Expectations*.

LITTLE DORRIT

Amy Dorrit, known to everyone as Little Dorrit, is the daughter of the debtor, William Dorrit. In *Little Dorrit*, Dickens drew on his childhood memories of life in Marshalsea, the debtor's prison. Although Dickens and his sister Fanny did not move into the prison with the rest of the family, he was a regular visitor to the prison while his family were there (see page 9). In the novel, Little Dorrit is born and brought up in the prison, and is eventually married in its shadow.

AN INNOCENT VICTIM

A brother and sister form the central child characters of Dickens's seventh novel, *Dombey and Son*. Florence Dombey is unloved by her father because she is a girl. Her younger brother, Paul, the longed-for heir, is a sickly child who dies during the course of the novel. Dickens wrote the death of Paul while living in Paris. '*I am slaughtering a young and innocent victim*' he reported in a letter. The episode of Paul's death was greeted with hysteria by Dickens's public. According to one observer, it '*flung a nation into mourning.*'

OLIVER TWIST

Oliver Twist is possibly Dickens' most famous book. Fleeing the brutality of Sowerberry the undertaker, Oliver goes to London and meets the boy thief, the Artful Dodger, and his gang, shown in this picture. Although Oliver's life is the focus of this novel, Dickens created some of his most memorable characters in the book, including Fagin, Sikes and Nancy.

FACT & FICTION

David Copperfield was Dickens's most popular novel and his personal favourite. It traces the life of David from his birth to his eventual marriage to Agnes. One of the autobiographical elements included in the story by Dickens was an episode in which, after his mother's death, David is forced to work in a warehouse, washing and labelling bottles. It is from this place that David flees to Dover, to throw himself on the mercy of his great-aunt, Betsy Trotwood (see page 17). This illustration shows David having tea at his great aunt's home.

LAISSEZ-FAIRE

In the 19th century, young children were employed to work in coal mines, as the illustration on the right shows. However, it was not until the Mines Act of 1842 that government attempted to put controls on dangerous working conditions. Until then, it was left up to employees and employers to sort out such matters between themselves – a policy known as 'laissez-faire'.

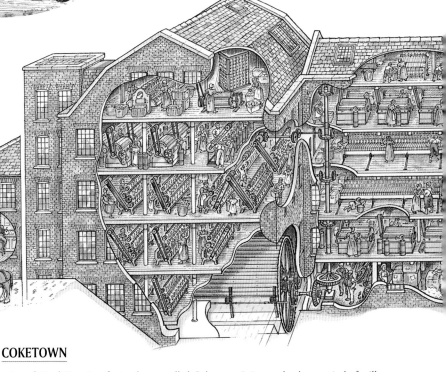

MR GRADGRIND

Through one of the central characters of *Hard Times*, Thomas Gradgrind, Dickens demonstrates what happens when the theory of Utilitarianism is put into practice. Mr Gradgrind believes in 'facts' and facts only – there is no room in his world for imagination or emotion. So, when Mr. Gradgrind asks for the definition of a horse, this is what he wants to hear: '*Quadruped. Graminivorous. Forty teeth, namely twenty-four grinders, four eye-teeth, and twelve incisive. Sheds coats in the spring; in marshy countries, sheds hoofs, too. Hoofs hard, but requiring to be shod with iron. Age known by marks in mouth.*'

COKETOWN

Dickens sets the action of *Hard Times* in a fictional town called Coketown. It is an ugly place, typical of mill towns and cities that developed during the Industrial Revolution, full of factories similar to the this 19th-century mill in Cheshire (above). Dickens describes Coketown as '*a town of red brick, that would have been red if the smoke and ashes had allowed it. . . It was a town of machinery and tall chimneys, out of which interminable serpents of smoke trailed themselves for ever and ever, and never got uncoiled.*'

DICKENS & THE INDUSTRIAL WORLD

Early in 1854, Dickens attended a meeting with his publishers. Receipts for *Household Words* (see page 13) were down, and the publishers felt a serialized story would help to revive sales. Dickens already had an idea for a new novel – and so *Hard Times* was born. It was published in weekly, not monthly, instalments, a schedule that Dickens found cripplingly difficult to keep to. Consequently, it is one of Dickens's shortest novels.

DICKENS vs. UTILITARIANISM

Dickens set *Hard Times* in the world of mechanized industry. One of his aims was to expose a system of thought called Utilitarianism, developed by the philosopher, Jeremy Bentham (shown above). The slogan of Utilitarianism was, *'It is the greatest happiness of the greatest number that is the measure of right or wrong'*, a theory that paid no regard to the distribution of benefits and burdens. But Dickens objected to Utilitarianism because he thought that it reduced humans to the status of machines, leaving no room for such unmeasurable qualities as imagination or emotion.

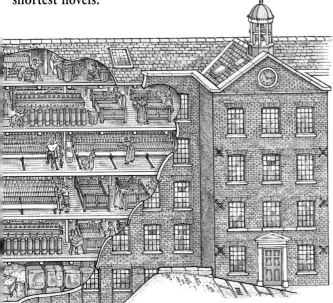

RESEARCHING HARD TIMES

In the cotton mills of northern England, children and women were used as cheap labour. Accidents were common as none of the machines had safety guards to protect the workers. Before starting work on *Hard Times*, Dickens did some research. He had already seen the factories and furnaces around Birmingham; in January 1854, he decided to visit Preston in Lancashire. There, the power-loom weavers from the cotton mills were on strike after a wage claim had been turned down by their employers. In reply, the mill owners had locked out all workers from their factories. Dickens attended a striker's meeting, and Preston provided much of the background detail for the novel. This poster illustrates the plight of such employees.

DICKENS & THE THEATRE

Ever since he was a child, Dickens loved everything to do with the theatre. As a youth in London he considered becoming a professional actor and approached the Covent Garden theatre for an audition. But when the day came, Dickens was ill '*with a terrible bad cold and an inflammation of the face*'. However, the theatre and acting continued to play an important part in Dickens's life.

CAPTAIN BOBADIL

Dickens retained his passion for the theatre throughout his adult life. In 1845, he and a group of friends put on a performance of *Every Man in His Humour* by the 17th-century English playwright, Ben Jonson. This painting shows Dickens in the role of Captain Bobadil. The play was performed at a small private theatre in Soho, and the audience included the poet, Alfred Tennyson (see page 7), and aristocrats such as the Duke of Devonshire.

STAGE-STRUCK

During the years that the Dickens family lived in Chatham, the young Charles was taken to see pantomime, featuring Harlequin and Columbine, as well as productions of Shakespeare's *Richard III* and *Macbeth*. He was also taken to see the great clown, Grimaldi (right). His interest in the theatre led him to write a play at the age of 10, 'Misnar, the Sultan of India' based on a story from *Tales of the Genii*, and to spend many hours playing with a small cut-out toy theatre and its characters.

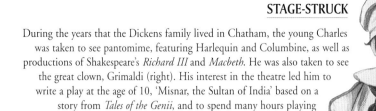

ACTING FOR THE QUEEN

Dickens often put on plays to raise money for fellow writers and artists. He loved everything to do with these performances, not only the acting itself, but also the organization of scenery and costumes, and the conviviality of being in a group of friends. He even took his performances on tours around the provinces. This picture shows a performance of *Not So Bad As We Seem* by Edward Bulwer Lytton, which was given before Queen Victoria in 1851.

THE DICKENS DRAMATIC COMPANY

This photograph shows the Dickens Dramatic Company in 1854. Charles Dickens is the reclining bearded figure at the front. Behind him is his eldest son, Charley, and to the right of him sit Kate Dickens, Georgina Hogarth and Mary Dickens. Wilkie Collins is the stooping figure to the left of Mary Dickens. Collins wrote one of the plays performed by the company, *The Frozen Deep*. It was on a tour of this play, in 1857, that Dickens met Ellen Ternan.

RAGGED SCHOOLS

In the 1820s, a movement started to give poor children a basic education. Run by volunteers (often self-educated themselves), these schools became known as Ragged Schools. Dickens became involved with the Ragged Schools in the 1840s, after visiting one of the schools in Holborn. He was appalled by the dilapidated state of the school, and the filth and stench of the children. Dickens's wealthy friend, Miss Burdett-Coutts duly provided money for better schoolrooms, and she remained involved in the Ragged School movement for the rest of her life.

DEBTOR'S PRISON

A debtor's prison provides the central location for much of the action in Dickens's eleventh novel *Little Dorrit*. Dickens wrote this work at a time when he was increasingly disillusioned with society in Britain. The indifference and selfishness of the wealthy, the corruption and inefficiency of government, and the lack of education and suffering of the poor brought him close to despair. In this frame of mind he created the Circumlocution Office in *Little Dorrit*, a government office whose purpose is *'How not to do it'*, and where nothing ever gets done.

LIFE IN THE WORKHOUSE

One of the earliest issues that Dickens tackled in his fiction was the treatment of children in workhouses like the one below in Alton in Staffordshire. Dickens was appalled by the introduction of the Poor Laws of 1834, and the opening chapters of his novel *Oliver Twist* were intended to draw attention to the suffering caused by these new measures. The new Poor Laws removed payments for able-bodied men and women. At the same time, conditions in the workhouses were made 'less eligible' – more prison-like. Families were split up, and the diet was reduced to cater for only the most basic needs.

A VOICE FOR THE POOR

Dickens knew only too well from his own childhood experiences what it was like to be poor. He was a lifelong campaigner for those who had no voice to speak for themselves, such as child chimney sweeps. He saw the need for better housing conditions, adequate sanitation and access to clean water. All these issues were well publicized in articles that appeared in Household Words *and* All The Year Round.

DICKENS & REFORM

ickens's years as a solicitor's clerk and parliamentary journalist left him deeply sceptical about the possibilities for reform through institutions such as the legal system or government. He preferred to set up projects such as Urania Cottage in Shepherd's Bush, London, a home for homeless women. He did this with the backing of Angela Burdett-Coutts's considerable fortune (*see page 12*), and oversaw the project for several years.

DOTHEBOY'S HALL

In 1838, Dickens made a brief trip to Yorkshire to see for himself one of the many boarding schools that had become notorious for their neglect and cruelty. Many children died as a result of their treatment at the hands of brutal teachers. Dickens went to a school in Bowes run by a man called William Shaw who, not surprisingly, was unwilling to help the novelist in his enquiries. But Dickens saw enough, and the result was the fictional Dotheboy's Hall (as illustrated above), the grim establishment in *Nicholas Nickleby* where Nicholas works as assistant to the sadistic Mr Squeers.

THE WRITER'S INFLUENCE

CHARLES DICKENS
BORN 7ᵀᴴ FEBRUARY 1812
DIED 9ᵀᴴ JUNE 1870

ickens's writing influenced many of his contemporaries, and has continued to inspire novelists ever since. But his influence was not confined to English writers and speakers. He was truly an international celebrity, and his novels were translated into many languages and read in many countries.

AN ENGLISH GENIUS

The death of Dickens sent people the world over into mourning. The American poet, Longfellow, remarked, *'It is no exaggeration to say that this whole country is stricken with grief.'* Dickens's status as a genius of English literature was immediately acknowledged by demands that he be buried not in Rochester, as he had requested, but in Poet's Corner in Westminster Abbey. An article in *The Times* confirmed the public mood: *'Westminster Abbey is the peculiar resting place of English Literary genius, and among those whose sacred dust lies there, very few are more worthy than Charles Dickens of such a home.'* He was buried in Westminster Abbey on 16th June 1870.

GEORGE GISSING

The novelist George Gissing was 13 when Dickens died. Gissing was greatly influenced by Dickens's writing, and dealt with similar subjects – the poor and the deprived – in many of his own novels. He wrote a study of Dickens's work (*Charles Dickens: A Critical Study*) in which he suggested that Dickens's genius lay in his ability to focus people's attention on serious issues through comedy: *'Only because they (the readers) laughed with him so heartily, did multitudes of people turn to discussing the question his page suggested.'* Gissing also shared Dickens's distrust of public institutions.

SCROOGE

Some of Dickens's characters have become famous personalities in their own right. One of his best-loved tales, *A Christmas Carol*, introduced the world to Scrooge, the miser. Mean-spirited, sneering and spiteful at the beginning of the book, by its end Scrooge is a changed man, made to comprehend the error of his ways by the ghosts of Christmas Past, Present and Future. His penny-pinching stinginess towards others, and in particular his employee Bob Cratchit, are eventually replaced by compassion and an understanding of the true meaning of Christmas. Today, he has become so much part of our literary heritage that the word 'Scrooge' is often used to describe a mean or miserly person.

RUSSIAN AUTHORS

Dickens's novels were read the world over, but there was a particular enthusiasm for his works in Russia. Leo Tolstoy, author of *War and Peace* (as dramatised here), read *David Copperfield* in translation and was so thrilled with Dickens's novel that he learned English in order to read it in the original language. Dickens was an influence on other Russian novelists, too, such as Fyodor Dostoevsky and Ivan Turgenev.

DICKENS'S BIOGRAPHER

Dickens's lifelong friend, John Forster, was a lawyer and writer. He wrote the first biography of Dickens (shown above), *The Life of Charles Dickens*. It was dedicated to his god-daughters Kate and Mary Dickens, and it omitted any possibly scandalous episodes in Dickens's life.

OLIVER!

The musical *Oliver!* was a huge hit when it opened in London in 1960, running for over 2,600 performances. It moved to Broadway, New York, in 1963. It was adapted by Lionel Bart, who also wrote the music. The musical was made into a film in 1968. This scene shows Fagin, played by Ron Moody, surrounded by his gang of boy pickpockets. The part of Oliver himself was played by Mark Lester.

A CHRISTMAS CAROL

Perhaps Dickens's most enduring novel is *A Christmas Carol*, which tells the story of the miser, Ebenezer Scrooge. The story has been brought to the screen on numerous occasions. Scrooge was played by Clive Francis (left) in the 1994 stage production of the book.

DICKENS ON FILM & IN THE THEATRE

At the time that Dickens was writing his novels, there was no copyright protection for authors. This meant that anyone could adapt or use texts without permission, without having to pay any fee to the author. Dickens spoke out against this practice many times. But there was little he could do about the many theatrical adaptations of his novels that were made during his lifetime. Often these adaptations dramatized only part of a novel or dispensed with some of the characters. The tradition of adapting Dickens's novels for the stage, and later for the screen, has continued ever since.

NICHOLAS NICKLEBY

This picture is of the BBC production of *Nicholas Nickleby*, starring Nigel Havers. Dickens's third novel includes such characters as Wackford Squeers, the owner of Dothebey's Hall, Smike, one of the miserable inhabitants of the school, the Crummles theatre company and the Cheerybles.

TV ADAPTATIONS

Dickens's novels have frequently been turned into adaptations for television, usually shown in several weekly episodes. *Our Mutual Friend* was made by the BBC and aired in 1998. It starred Anna Friel as Bella Wilfer, Steven Mackintosh as John Harmon and Timothy Spall as Mr Venus. One critic said: *'Julian Farino, the director of* Our Mutual Friend, *has taken a huge sprawling novel by the scruff of the neck and turned it into a work of art for television.'*

GREAT EXPECTATIONS

Sometimes the plot of a novel is used simply as the basis for a film. This is what happened with the 1998 production of *Great Expectations*. Although the film retained Dickens's original title, and used his plot as a starting point, the action was updated to modern-day New York City, and the names of the characters were different from those in the book. Ethan Hawke played 'Finn' – Finnegan Bell – in a story of love for an unobtainable woman, Estella, played by Gwyneth Paltrow.

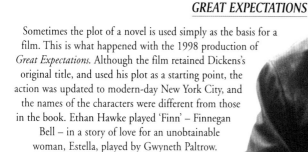

DID YOU KNOW?

Dickens was a very restless person, with seemingly endless energy. He used to walk for miles, often covering distances of 20 or 30 miles at a time.

Twenty years after she rejected him, Dickens's first love, Maria Beadnell, wrote to the famous author. The two former lovers decided to meet, but Dickens was appalled at how much Maria had changed, despite her warning him that she was now '*fat, old, and ugly*'. Dickens recreated the old Maria in the character of Flora in Little Dorrit.

In 1865, Dickens was given an unusual present by a Swiss friend and admirer, the actor Charles Fechter. It was a Swiss chalet – a real, full-size one – in 94 pieces. Dickens had it assembled in the garden of Gad's Hill Place, and he often worked in it during warmer summer months.

Dickens was such a celebrity during his first tour of America that people waited alongside the railway on which he was travelling to catch a glimpse of the famous author. Dickens quickly grew tired of the endless publicity, however. He reported: '*I can't… drink a glass of water, without having a hundred people looking down my throat when I open my mouth to swallow…*'

As a child, Dickens often passed the forbidding walls of Newgate Prison in London, where the bodies of recently hanged criminals were displayed. Later in his life, he attended a public hanging at the same prison.

When he died, Dickens left his last novel, *The Mystery of Edwin Drood*, unfinished. No one knows how he intended to complete this tale, so Edwin's disappearance remains a mystery to this day.

ACKNOWLEDGEMENTS

We would like to thank Elizabeth Wiggans for her assistance and David Hobbs for his illustration of Quarry Bank Mill.
Copyright © 2001 *ticktock* Publishing Ltd, Century Place, Lamberts Road, Tunbridge Wells, Kent, TN2 3EH
First published in Great Britain by ticktock Publishing Ltd., Great Britain. All rights reserved.
No part of this publication may be reproduced, stored in a retrieval system, or transmitted in any form
or by any means electronic, mechanical, photocopying, recording or otherwise, without prior written
permission of the copyright owner.

A CIP catalogue record for this book is available from the British Library. ISBN 1 86007 241 0 (pbk) 186007 243 7 (hbk)